Anchored

A Journey Through Vision and Faith

By

Trey Lewis

Copyright © 2025 by Trey Lewis

All rights reserved.

No part of this book may be reproduced, distributed, or transmitted in any form or by any means, including photocopying, recording, or other electronic or mechanical methods, without the prior written permission of the publisher, except in the case of brief quotations embodied in reviews, critical articles, or certain other noncommercial uses permitted by copyright law.

Cover Design by NH Arafat

Layout Design by NH Arafat

Contents

Introduction 1

Chapter 1: *A Name I Didn't Choose* 6

Chapter 2: *A New Battle* 17

Chapter 3: *Parkview Bound* 29

Chapter 4: *A Town, A Life, A Journey Through Limitations* 38

Chapter 5: *Seizures and Second Chances* 49

Chapter 6: *Finding My Lane on Campus* 61

Chapter 7: *The Hollow Places* 75

Chapter 8: *The Unexpected Friendship* 86

Chapter 9: *The Valley Season* 98

Chapter 10: *Never Say Never* 108

Chapter 11: *Anchored in Faith and Connections* 119

INTRODUCTION

Welcome Aboard

L ife, I've learned, is a lot like sailing a ship out at sea. One minute, you're cruising through calm waters with the sun kissing your face and the breeze gently pushing you forward. The next minute—bam! —you're caught in a raging storm, gripping the wheel for dear life, wondering if you'll make it out in one piece. The rudder won't budge, the horizon disappears, and you start to believe your ship might just crash into oblivion.

Those are the moments that test you—the dark and choppy nights when it's hard to stay focused or find anything positive on the radar. But after 34 years of sailing, I've come to realize something: those storms teach you things. Not always fun things, but important ones. Lessons that prepare you for whatever waves might come next. And once you've weathered one or two of those tempests, you start learning how to navigate future ones a little better. Or at least, you keep the bucket handy when the water comes in.

Sometimes, you don't realize how strong your ship is until the storm comes. I've had times when I thought the mast would snap clean off—when the fear of sinking felt louder than any voice of hope. But you find a way. Maybe it's grit. Maybe it's grace. Maybe it's a little of both. You learn to patch the holes while the water's still pouring in. And somehow, you keep sailing.

My name is Brandon Trey Lewis—but please, just call me Trey. Over the next few pages, you're going to read about my journey through some pretty rough waters. From being diagnosed with a disease and beginning to lose my sight at the age of six, to carving out a career I'm proud of today. This is the story of how I kept my ship afloat with the help of Faith, Family, and a whole crew of Friends.

Let me take you back to the beginning for a second. I was just a kid when the world shifted beneath my feet. One doctor visit, one unexpected diagnosis, and suddenly the colors started to dim. I didn't know then that it would change everything. I didn't know that simple things like crossing the street or finding my classroom would become daily challenges. But I knew this: I had people who believed in me. And I had a quiet fire in me that wasn't going to be put out easily.

Now, let's be clear—I never set out to write a book. I didn't wake up one day and say, "You know what the world needs? My story." But I do believe there's power in shared experience. If you're in the middle of your own storm, I want you to know you're not alone, and you can make it through. I'm not writing this so you'll feel sorry for me, or think I'm some kind of superhero. Trust me, I still trip over my own feet (and occasionally walk into furniture). I'm just a regular guy who's learned that, sometimes, life's greatest strength is built when things get messy.

Maybe your storm looks nothing like mine. Maybe it's a heartbreak. Maybe it's an addiction. Maybe it's just waking up every day feeling like the tide is always pulling you under. Whatever it is, I hope this book gives you something to hold on to—a little hope, a little laughter, maybe even a moment where you feel seen. You don't have to be perfect to keep sailing. You just have to stay in the boat.

People like to assume that those of us with disabilities can't do much—that we're limited or fragile. Well, I'm here to tell you that's nonsense. You might have to work a little harder, get your hands dirty, and take a few unexpected detours, but it's absolutely possible to thrive. And sometimes, the journey gets better because of the mess, not in spite of it.

Before we dive into the rest of the story, I want to recognize the crew that's kept me afloat. No sailor survives the sea alone—and I've been blessed with the best.

First, to my parents, Brandon and Regina Lewis: You are the very definition of unconditional love. You've sacrificed more than I could ever list and cheered me on every step of the way. Sure, you're a little crazy—but then again, so am I. Love you both more than words.

To my grandparents: Bobby Presgrove (Granny), Sandy Carter (Grandma), Adrain Lewis, and the late Jerry Presgrove (Papa), Rex Lewis (Old Man), and Harv Carter (Grandpa). You've shown me love, support, and plenty of prayers. I carry your strength with me every day. Granny once told me, "Don't pray for calm seas, pray for a stronger boat." That stuck. Especially on the days when the waves felt bigger than me.

To my aunts, uncles, and cousins, too many to name individually, but every one of you has played a major role in my life. Thank you, and I love you all.

To my friends: You've inspired me, included me, and stood by me regardless of my disability. Some of you have been around for years, others just for a season, but every moment we've shared is something I cherish. You laughed with me when I fell, and you pulled me up when I couldn't see the way forward. That matters.

I want to take a moment to thank the doctors who have stood by me and my family. They've walked with us through some of the roughest seasons—offering more than just medical help. They gave us compassion, presence, and guidance when we didn't know what was coming next.

And to Samuel—thank you for taking on the challenge of helping me tell my story. Your ability to capture my voice, with nothing but our message threads to guide you, has been nothing short of amazing. You've brought structure, clarity, and care to something deeply personal, and I'm grateful for the respect you've shown my experiences every step of the way.

This book isn't just about the diagnosis or the procedures. It's about faith, resilience, and the people who've helped carry the load when it got too heavy. You're part of that story now too.

And finally, to you—the reader: Thank you for picking up this book. I'm not famous, I'm not a CEO, I'm not a millionaire. I'm a public servant with a story to tell and a heart full of hope. I pray that as you read these pages, you find encouragement, laughter, and maybe even a little peace. Let's set sail together—and see where this journey takes us.

CHAPTER 1

A Name I Didn't Choose

Click, click, click. Knock, knock. Buzz, buzz, buzz, buzz. Repeat for the next 90 minutes. That sound is all too familiar to me. It's the rhythmic hum and rattle of a machine I've known most of my life—though it sounds quite different now than it did thirty years ago. You must have guessed it right: an MRI, or Magnetic Resonance Imaging machine.

I've been having MRIs since I was just three years old. Back then, the experience was very different. The scans took nearly an hour and a half, and there was no music—just the cold, mechanical clatter echoing through the room. My most recent MRI? It took only about 20 minutes, and I got to listen to music the entire time. That, my friend, is a game changer.

Over the years, I've been told I've had just about every type of brain scan ever developed. CT scans. PET scans. EEGs. MRIs, of course. You name it—I've probably had it. We'll get into more of that later in this book. But for now, just know that these machines have been with me through nearly every phase of life. They've become part of the background noise, the medical soundtrack accompanying my story.

So, why all the scans? I was diagnosed with Neurofibromatosis Type 1 (NF1) when I was three years old, a diagnosis that would go on to shape my childhood and much of my life in ways I never could have imagined.

Neurofibromatosis Type 1 is a genetic condition that affects about 1 in every 3,000 people worldwide, making it one of the most common inherited neurological disorders. But just because it's common doesn't mean it's easy. Far from it.

One significant aspect of NF1 is that nearly half of those diagnosed—myself included—don't inherit it from a parent. In those cases, it results from a spontaneous genetic mutation. That's science-speak for: one day, the genetic blueprint took a hard left turn and rewrote the instructions. No warning. No manual. No going back. That's where my journey began.

After receiving my diagnosis, my parents sprang into action. Back then, the internet wasn't what it is today. There were no support groups online, no accessible YouTube videos breaking down the complexities. They leaned on doctors, medical pamphlets, and pure grit. They did everything they could to understand what we were facing and how best to navigate it.

Some people with NF1 develop visible tumors on or under the skin, while others experience internal growths. Some deal with scoliosis. Others have learning difficulties or speech delays. Some have eye or vision problems, while others struggle with chronic pain. I'm grateful that I haven't had to deal with all of these symptoms—but that didn't mean the road was smooth.

At the time, all I really knew was that I went to more doctor appointments than most kids my age—and I endured more medical tests and procedures, too. Needles. Machines. Long waits in sterile hospital rooms. Specialists whose names I couldn't pronounce and whose faces blurred together. That was normal for me. That was childhood.

Through those early years, my family was the anchor that kept everything steady. My parents did their best to remain calm, even when the future seemed uncertain. They carried a weight I couldn't comprehend at the time, and they shielded me from most of it. They didn't panic in front of me, even when their own hearts were probably breaking. Looking back now, I can see how much strength it must have taken. I'm still in awe of it.

My cousins and I were all still young, and they didn't fully grasp what was happening either. To them, I was just Trey. We played together, watched cartoons, chased each other through backyards. For a while, things felt normal. That window of innocence, however brief, gave me something to hold onto. In those moments, I didn't feel like a patient. I just felt like a kid.

As for me? From what I've been told—and from watching old home videos—I acted like any typical 3- or 4-year-old boy. Always trying to make people laugh, no matter the setting. Always dancing when music played, no matter the genre. Music has always been, and continues to be, the driving force running through my DNA. It wasn't just something I enjoyed—it was something that gave me energy, a kind of internal compass.

Music became an outlet. When everything else felt out of my control—doctors poking and prodding, schedules filled with appointments I didn't understand, adults speaking in hushed, worried tones—music made sense. It didn't require a diagnosis or a scan or a label. It just was. I could sing. I could listen. I could feel. I could escape. And sometimes, escape was exactly what I needed.

Eventually, the doctor visits became part of the background, and I started school. That was a transition. I was nervous—about leaving the safety of home, about being around new people who didn't know anything about MRIs or NF1 or why I had so many appointments. But just as we began to find our rhythm and steady the rudder, something else knocked us off course.

What came next wasn't expected. Not by my parents. Not by the doctors. Not even by the specialists who had studied this condition for years. My vision began to change. It started slowly, subtly. A little more squinting. A little more holding books closer to my face. Then street signs got harder to read. Colors dimmed. And then came the undeniable truth: I was losing my sight.

It wasn't just another symptom. It was a major shift. A transformation I had no control over. And like every other twist in this medical journey, we had to learn as we went. There was no medicine to fix it. No surgery to reverse it. Just the reality of what was happening.

My family rallied around me, like they always did. But no amount of preparation can soften the emotional blow of losing something you didn't even know you were clinging to so tightly. My sight—this thing most people never even think about—was slipping away. And I couldn't stop it. None of us could.

I remember feeling frustrated. Not just by the diagnosis or the limitations, but by the helplessness. The loss of control. I didn't have the vocabulary at the time to explain it, but I could feel the shift. I could feel the weight of being different. And I began to sense how others were starting to see me differently too.

That's when the label began to stick. The one I never asked for. The one that began to override the name I'd been building for myself—funny, musical, resilient little Trey. That's when I became, in the eyes of some, "the blind kid." "The disabled one."

That's the name I didn't choose.

People adjusted their behavior. Some out of concern. Some out of ignorance. Some simply didn't know how to act around me anymore. And as those interactions piled up, so did the weight of it all. The accommodations, the special treatment, the pity—it was all well-intentioned, but it wasn't always helpful. Sometimes, it just reminded me of what I had lost. Of what was different.

But even in those difficult moments, there were glimmers of light. A teacher who treated me with dignity, not pity. A friend who didn't flinch or speak to me like I was fragile. A cousin who still saw me as just Trey. These people helped me feel grounded when everything else was shifting. They reminded me of who I was beyond the diagnosis.

I didn't fully understand the road ahead, but I knew this much: my story wasn't over. It was only just beginning. While I didn't get to choose the name that came with my diagnosis, I could still choose how I responded to it. I could choose to keep showing up. To fight. To find joy. To laugh, even when it hurt. To keep moving forward, even when the path ahead was unclear.

And that, I've learned, is sometimes more than enough.

Take Away:

Life doesn't always give you the script you expect—but with resilience, support, and a sense of humor, you can still write a powerful story.

When I think about that first chapter of my life—the sound of the MRI machine, the diagnosis, the constant visits to doctors—I think about the things I didn't get to choose. I didn't choose NF1. I didn't choose the countless hours in sterile hospital rooms or the silent stares from people who didn't know what to say. I didn't choose the label that followed me like a second name. And yet, all those things shaped me. Maybe not by choice—but certainly by force, and later, by intention.

I used to think the most defining moment of my childhood was the diagnosis itself. But looking back now, I realize it wasn't the diagnosis. It was what came after. It was the way my parents, scared and uncertain, still found a way to hold it together. It was the way they taught me, not through lectures but through presence, that you can still show up when life knocks you down. That love doesn't always look like big speeches or grand gestures—it often looks like a hand holding yours in the waiting room.

That kind of love is the quiet kind. The kind that doesn't demand applause. And it's the kind that kept me steady, even when everything around me was changing.

When you're a kid, you don't always have the language to describe what's happening to you. You just feel it. You feel the difference before you understand it. You sense the worry in adult voices, the hesitation in other children, the shift in the air when people look at you. And slowly, without even realizing it, you begin to internalize a new script—a new identity. One that wasn't yours to begin with.

"Disabled." That word entered my life long before I understood what it meant. It wasn't just a descriptor. It became a lens. A filter that people used when they saw me, when they spoke to me, when they tried to decide what I was capable of. And for a while, I didn't push back. I wore it like a second skin because I didn't know I had the right to shed it—or at least redefine it on my own terms.

But that's the thing about growing up. You start to see your own power. You start to understand that you may not have chosen the story you were handed, but you do get to choose what you do with it. And for me, that choice came in the form of music, laughter, and refusal. Refusal to be boxed in. Refusal to be pitied. Refusal to be underestimated.

Music was the first language I truly understood. It didn't ask questions. It didn't need explanations. It just was. No matter how many MRIs or vision tests I had to endure, I could always come back to a melody, a beat, a harmony that made sense when nothing else did. Music didn't see me as broken. It didn't whisper about accommodations or special needs. It welcomed me, just as I was.

And laughter—well, laughter was my rebellion. My way of saying, "You don't get to write me off." It was how I reclaimed the room, how I softened the edges of difficult moments, how I reminded myself and others that I was still here. Still funny. Still full of light.

As I reflect on those early years, I think about the innocence I had—the freedom of not yet understanding how cruel or careless the world could be. I think that innocence protected me. It gave me space to just be, to live in the moment without being crushed by the weight of it all. And yet, I also think about the moment that innocence began to fade—the slow dimming of the world as my vision began to change.

There's a particular kind of grief that comes from losing something you never expected to lose. Sight is something most people take for granted. You open your eyes and expect the world to greet you in full color. When that starts to fade, you grieve not just the loss itself but the future you thought you were heading toward. You grieve the version of yourself that could see the world clearly—and all the possibilities that came with that.

But here's what I've learned: grief and growth are not mutually exclusive. You can mourn what was while still reaching for what could be. You can cry and laugh in the same breath. You can feel broken and still be whole.

NF1 taught me that. Not all at once, and not easily. But eventually. It taught me that you don't have to be fearless to be brave. You don't have to be strong all the time to be resilient. You just have to keep going. Even when it's hard. Especially when it's hard.

People often ask me how I've stayed positive, how I've kept my sense of humor. And the truth is—I haven't always. There were dark days. There were moments of bitterness, of anger, of wanting to scream at the universe for being so unfair. But I learned to sit with those feelings, to let them pass through without building a home inside me. Because as valid as those feelings are, they're not the whole story.

The whole story is this: I'm still here. I'm still writing. Still creating. Still laughing. Still living. And that means something.

This chapter—this beginning—was not the one I would've written for myself. But it's mine. And owning it has given me the freedom to write the rest of my story on my own terms.

I don't know what challenges lie ahead. I don't know what parts of myself I'll lose or gain along the way. But I do know this: I am more than a diagnosis. I am more than a name I didn't choose. I am a storyteller, a musician, a son, a friend. And no condition, no matter how rare or complex, gets to take that away from me.

So, if you're reading this and you've ever felt defined by something you didn't choose—a diagnosis, a label, a circumstance—I want you to know: you are not alone. And you are not powerless.

You may not get to choose the opening lines of your story, but you do get to choose what comes next. How you show up. What you fight for. What you believe about yourself. And those choices? They are everything.

Because life doesn't always give you the script you expect—but with resilience, support, and a sense of humor, you can still write a powerful story and I plan to keep writing mine.

CHAPTER 2

A New Battle

I began school in Comanche, Oklahoma—a small one-stoplight town tucked away in the southwest corner of the state. It was the kind of place where everyone knew your name, your story, and probably what you were doing before you did it. In Comanche, life revolved around three things: sports, family, and church. My mom's side of the family, the Presgroves, was one of the largest in town. If you asked anyone who knew us, they'd say the same thing—we're loud, we're wild, and we love hard. We may not always like each other, but mess with one of us and you'd better be ready to deal with the whole herd.

Despite the town's size, I found a strong community—friends from school and church who became like brothers and sisters to me. Life was simple back then, and for the most part, it was a great childhood. We spent hours in the pool playing Marco Polo, laughing until we couldn't breathe, shouting each other's names across the water like it was our own version of a battlefield. There was something about small-town childhood that made you believe, even if just for a little while, that everything would be okay.

Around the age of five, I started playing sports. First soccer, then T-ball. That's when things started to feel… off. I remember standing out on the field and hearing my parents—and the other parents in the stands—shouting, "Trey! Keep your eye on the ball!"

What none of us knew at the time was that I couldn't see the ball. I wasn't careless or distracted, I was going blind. But I didn't know that. I was six years old. At that age, you just assume the world looks the same to everyone. I had no idea my vision was slipping away. But we were about to find out why.

"Your son has an optic glioma tumor that's grown on his optic nerve."

Those words came out of the ophthalmologist's mouth like a hammer. They changed everything. That doctor—one we'd grow to trust and love—was the first and only medical professional I've ever met who closed every session with a prayer. I'll never forget that.

I was too young to fully grasp the weight of the diagnosis, but I can only imagine how it hit my parents. Shock. Fear. Confusion. What do we do now? Where do we go from here? All I remember is watching their faces tighten. There were no tears in that room. Not then. But there was something unspoken. Like they knew our lives had just divided into two parts: before the tumor, and after.

That day marked the beginning of a new battle—one I never saw coming. But battles don't scare me. They shape me.

What's wild is that only a small percentage of people with NF1 develop this kind of tumor. Of those who do, not all experience vision loss. So if this was the hardest symptom I'd have to face, I considered myself lucky. Sure, it wasn't fair. But life isn't fair, and fairness isn't promised. We don't get to pick the battles—we just get to decide how we'll fight them.

After those words, we were shocked for a few days, but we knew what we had to do. We continued to rely on faith, family, and friends to get us through the rough waters ahead. And those waters? They got choppy. Fast. But like every person out at sea, you need a good crew to help keep you afloat. My crew? They showed up. My family was there every step of the way. My church community? Present. Neighbors and friends? On board.

We didn't really have much time to grieve—we went straight into more medical testing. I had a brain biopsy shortly after the diagnosis. Then I had a port implanted in my side so I could begin chemotherapy.

I was in first grade when the chemo started. That's also when the teasing began at my public school. Although I don't remember every insult or sideways glance, I vaguely remember the playground. The way kids stared. The way I suddenly felt different. It was heartbreaking, but I did my best to continue living life as normally as possible. My parents tried to shield me from the worst of it, but kids can sense when something is off. And I knew I was off.

The chemo was rough. The port in my side hurt when I moved too fast. I felt tired all the time. My appetite disappeared. But I kept going to school. I kept showing up. Not because I had to, but because I wanted to. I didn't want this thing to take more from me than it already had.

During that time, I had an unforgettable experience with the Make-A-Wish Foundation. A woman came to the hospital and asked what I would wish for. That was a big question for a six-year-old! I considered meeting a celebrity, but in the end, I chose Disney—and it was a trip I'll never forget.

We went to Disney World, skipped to the front of every ride, stayed at a resort, and even visited Universal Studios, where I got slimed. This was the 90s, and back then, every kid dreamed of getting slimed! That trip was unforgettable, and I am truly thankful for this amazing organization. Years later, after I graduated college, I had the chance to help grant wishes through the same foundation. Life really does come full circle.

Eventually, the doctors told us they had managed to shrink the tumor by 50 percent. That was huge. Monumental, even. In a world full of scans and setbacks, this felt like a win—a real one. We celebrated the way people who've been holding their breath for too long do. With tears, laughter, and quiet gratitude that ran deeper than words. There was a collective exhale in my house that day. Finally, something had gone our way.

But—because there always seems to be a "but"—there was a catch. The vision I had already lost? That was gone for good. No surgery or pill could bring it back. We had stopped the bleeding, but the damage had already been done. And at that age, maybe seven years old, that was hard to wrap my head around. I didn't really understand how something could be good news and bad news all at once. How a victory could still carry a loss. It didn't seem fair. Then again, most of what had happened so far hadn't been fair.

A lot of people have asked me over the years what I actually see. It's a fair question, and honestly, it's hard to explain. My right eye? It's like looking through a straw—maybe a little bigger than a coffee straw—but with layers of saran wrap covering the end. Just a blurry, cloudy tunnel. And my left eye? All I can really see is hand motion right up against my nose. That's it. That's my normal.

At that time, I was learning—fast and early—that life doesn't follow a neat, predictable storyline. There's no straight line from pain to progress. It's more like a puzzle where some pieces don't fit, and others are missing altogether. Life is messy. Complicated. Bittersweet. You win some ground, and you lose something else in the process. You take a step forward and realize you've left something important behind.

Still, in the middle of all that complexity, one truth stood out: we had weathered a serious storm. I had made it through chemotherapy. Through long nights in hospital beds and early mornings filled with needles and IV drips. Through the confusion, the exhaustion, the frustration. Through all of it, I had made it out on the other side. Sure, my sight would never be the same—but I was here. Alive. Breathing. Laughing, even and that counted for something.

No, scratch that—that counted for everything.

Sometimes we look for huge miracles, the kind that make headlines or fill up church pews. But the fact that I was still standing, still smiling, still moving forward? That was a miracle all on its own. But if there's one thing life had taught me by then, it was this: storms don't ask for your permission before they roll in. You don't get to rest for too long. Just when you think the sun's coming out, the clouds start gathering again.

Another storm was already on its way. We didn't know it yet—not fully—but the next chapter of my life wasn't going to be easier just because I'd gotten through this one. That's the thing people don't always say out loud: Surviving something hard doesn't exempt you from more hard things.

It just means you've got experience now. Scars that prove you've fought before—and that you can fight again.

My journey into adolescence was waiting. And with it came a whole new set of challenges. Bigger questions. Heavier emotions. That space between being a kid and becoming something more. That's where I was headed next. But something had changed in me.

I wasn't just a scared little kid anymore. I had faced something terrifying and walked through it. I had learned that pain doesn't mean you're broken. That loss doesn't mean your story is over. That joy and sorrow can live side by side. And maybe most important of all, I was learning that survival—while important—was never meant to be the end goal. Surviving isn't the end of the story. It's just the beginning of the next chapter.

A chapter where I'd learn to live with purpose. To carry what I'd lost without letting it define me. To find new ways to move through a world that sometimes felt blurry, both literally and figuratively. A chapter where I'd dig deeper, grow stronger in my faith, and learn what it means to trust God.

Take Away:

You Can't Choose the Storm, But You Can Choose Your Crew

If I've learned anything from those early years, it's this: you don't get to choose the storm, but you do get to choose who's in your boat. And when the waters rise, that crew—the people rowing with you, praying with you, showing up when it's ugly and inconvenient—they make all the difference. I didn't get a say in my diagnosis. I didn't ask for the tumor. I definitely didn't sign up to lose part of my vision as a six-year-old kid just trying to play T-ball and eat dinosaur nuggets. But what I did get to choose—what we all get to choose—is how we respond. And who we walk with.

That's something I didn't fully understand back then, but I see it now. It wasn't just me fighting this. My parents were in it. My family. My friends. My doctors. My church. There were people showing up to help. People bringing casseroles when my mom was too exhausted to cook. My classmates—some of them, at least—who stood by me even when I looked or felt different. And of course, there was God.

Let's talk about Him for a second.

There's a passage in the Bible that has always stuck with me—John 9. It's the story of Jesus healing a man who had been blind from birth. When Jesus and his disciples came across him, the disciples asked a question that sounds a lot like something I think many people wondered about me too: "Rabbi, who sinned, this man or his parents, that he was born blind?"

Isn't that just like us humans? We want reasons. We want blame. We want something that makes sense of the pain. But

Jesus doesn't give them that. Instead, He says, "Neither this man nor his parents sinned, but this happened so that the works of God might be displayed in him."

That verse rocked me. Still does.

See, I believe Jesus can heal. If He wanted to, He could restore every inch of my vision in a second. I believe that with my whole heart. But here's what I also believe—He didn't have to heal me in the way I thought He should in order to use me in the way He planned. Just like that man in John 9, my story has never been about punishment or brokenness. It's about purpose.

That's a hard truth to swallow when you're a kid who just wants to see the ball like everyone else. It's confusing. It hurts. There were days I begged God to fix it. Nights I cried and asked why He'd let this happen. And you know what? He never gave me the kind of answer I was hoping for.

Instead, He gave me people.

He gave me parents who were my fiercest advocates. He gave me doctors who fought for me. Nurses who cared like I was their own. Friends who didn't let the blindness define me. Pastors who reminded me that faith isn't about everything making sense—it's about trusting when it doesn't.

He gave me a crew.

That's what I mean when I say the worst moments in life reveal your deepest support systems. When the lights go out and the storm comes crashing through, you start to see who really shows up. You learn who's in it for the long haul. And that changes you.

It also humbles you.

Because the truth is, I couldn't have done any of this alone. I needed people. I needed help. And I think that's one of the greatest lies we're told—that strength means doing it all on your own. That's not strength. That's pride. Real strength is knowing when to reach out. It's saying, "I need you." It's trusting others to carry some of the weight when your own arms are tired.

There's something sacred about being weak and letting someone else help you stand.

I didn't know it back then, but that lesson would shape the rest of my life. Every major battle that came after—from surgeries to setbacks to new diagnoses—was faced with the same mindset: I don't have to do this alone.

But let's be clear. That doesn't mean I never doubted.

There were seasons when I was angry. Bitter, even. Times when I watched my friends do things I couldn't—ride bikes with no fear, play sports without accommodation, run freely without needing someone to guide them. I'd sit in those moments and wonder, "Why me?" And if you're reading this and you've asked that question too, I just want to say—I get it. It's okay. You're not wrong for asking. And you're not alone in that question.

But here's what I've also found: the "why" isn't always the point. Sometimes the better question is, "What now?" What do I do with what I've been given? How do I make something meaningful out of something painful? What story can I tell that might give someone else hope?

Making it through chemotherapy was one thing. Losing my vision and learning to live with that was another. But choosing to live fully—to keep dreaming, to keep laughing, to keep showing up even when things are hard—that's where the real victory is.

Sometimes I think, maybe that's the greater miracle. Not just being healed, but being whole. Not just getting through it, but growing through it.

My life may look different than I imagined. But it's not less. It's more layered. More textured. More real. And I wouldn't trade the relationships, the resilience, or the faith I've found for a few extra pixels of eyesight.

I don't need to see perfectly to see clearly. And what I see is this:

Storms will come. You can't avoid them. You can't control them. But you can choose your crew. You can surround yourself with people who will steady your boat when the waves hit hard. And if you're lucky—and I am—you'll find that God often shows up not as a sudden miracle, but as the quiet strength in the people who never leave your side.

That's what I want you to take from this chapter. Not that life is fair. Not that everything always works out the way you'd hoped. But that you're never alone. That faith isn't the absence of struggle—it's the decision to keep showing up anyway. And that healing sometimes comes in the form of being held, not fixed.

So yeah, I still believe God can heal me. But if He chooses not to, I trust that it's because He's doing something even greater with my story. That kind of faith doesn't come easy. But it comes from living it. From walking through fire and realizing you're not walking alone. And if you're going through something right now—if you feel like you're in the middle of your own storm—look around. Who's in your boat? Who's helping you row? Don't focus so much on calming the waves that you miss the miracle of the people beside you. That's where you'll find your strength. That's where you'll find your story. And like me, you may just find that what you thought was the end... was really just the beginning.

CHAPTER 3

Parkview Bound

Toward the end of my first-grade year, I vaguely remember a lady coming to meet with me at school. She assessed me using bold-line paper, a Sharpie-like pen that wouldn't bleed through, and began introducing me to embossed shapes and dots. I didn't know it at the time, but that meeting marked the beginning of my blindness training. It felt strange, almost like I was being shown a secret code that the rest of my classmates didn't know about. At that age, I didn't have the language for it, but I sensed that my life was about to take a different path from most of the kids I knew.

While I was meeting with her, my parents were speaking with someone else about the possibility of sending me to the Oklahoma School for the Blind—a residential K-12 school for blind and visually impaired students, located in Muskogee, Oklahoma. My parents didn't want to hear it at first. They wanted me to stay in public school, to have the same kind of childhood they thought every kid deserved. But after some conversation, and no doubt with heavy hearts, they agreed to enroll me in a summer program there. It was a decision they didn't make lightly, because it wasn't just about me—it meant changing how our whole family functioned.

I don't remember much from those two weeks of the summer program, but I do know I didn't like it. I was away from my friends, away from my familiar surroundings, and at the end of the day, it was still school. Even in summer, I was being taught, tested, and evaluated. For a kid my age, that was not my idea of fun. I counted the days until I could go home. When the summer ended, my parents decided to let me continue attending public school, and I was relieved. That relief lasted… until second grade.

"We're moving to Muskogee so you can attend Parkview, also known as the Oklahoma School for the Blind." Those were the words my mom said to me. I didn't want to go. In my young mind, it felt like my whole world was ending. I didn't want to leave my friends and family behind. I didn't want to trade the familiar streets, voices, and routines of my hometown for something unknown. Muskogee was three hours away from everything I knew. At that age, three hours felt like another planet.

Now that I'm an adult, I'm incredibly grateful for the sacrifices my parents made—grateful in a way I couldn't fully understand as a child. My dad kept working as a fireman in Oklahoma City, making the long commute back and forth 10 days each month. The mileage, the hours, the constant disruption to his own rest and routine—it was no small thing.

He gave up time at home, comfort, and stability so that I could have a chance at something better. My mom, meanwhile, had to uproot her life, adapt to a completely new community, and figure out how to make it feel like home. All the while, she made sure I had not just the basics, but what I truly needed to succeed. Their sacrifices weren't only about getting me an education—they were about equipping me with the skills, mindset, and resilience to live independently and confidently in a world that isn't always designed with people like me in mind.

When I started attending Parkview, I was surrounded by people like me, although I didn't realize that at first. It was the first place I'd ever been where blindness wasn't unusual, where adaptive tools were part of everyday life instead of exceptions. That sense of belonging was subtle but powerful. Still, that didn't mean the transition was easy. I had to relearn everything I'd already been taught in public school—but this time, I had to learn it through a completely different lens, as a blind student. Reading, writing, moving through hallways—all the things most kids take for granted—had to be approached in ways that worked for me. It wasn't just about learning academics anymore; it was about learning systems, techniques, and confidence in a whole new form.

One thing I've always been clear about is that I never wanted to be seen as "the blind kid." In my own mind, I was simply a normal kid who happened to be blind, and I resisted anything that might set me apart more than I already felt. I didn't want to read Braille, I didn't want to use a cane, and I certainly didn't want to embrace the "blind things" that, at the time, felt like labels. I've always been a little stubborn—ask anyone who knows me, and they'll tell you I don't change my mind easily. It took both of my parents, with equal parts patience, persistence, and quiet insistence, to push me to learn Braille. At the time, I didn't understand why they cared so much. Eventually, though, I began to see its value—not just as a skill, but as a lifeline to independence. Now, I'm its biggest advocate. I tell anyone who will listen how important it is, because I've lived the difference it makes.

The cane, on the other hand, took a very different kind of persuasion. I resisted it for years, avoiding it whenever possible. And then one day, an unexpected moment made me see it differently. I was in middle school, walking through a mall in Tulsa with a friend, holding his elbow in what's called a human guide. People kept glancing at us as they passed, and while I couldn't fully interpret their expressions, I felt a strange tension. Through gritted teeth, my friend whispered, "Trey, let go and walk beside me. Your dad is ahead." When we caught up to my dad, my friend told me matter-of-factly, "Trey, everyone was looking at us like we were a couple." The realization landed hard. In that moment, I understood that my reluctance to use a cane was shaping how people perceived me in ways I didn't intend. That was the wake-up call I needed. I learned then that sometimes change doesn't come because someone lectures you or patiently reasons with you—it comes when life catches you off guard and forces you to see yourself through a different lens.

At school, I also began learning how to cook, clean, and handle the basic daily living tasks that sighted people often take for granted. I learned to measure ingredients by touch, to organize my clothes so I could tell them apart, to navigate unfamiliar buildings using memory and sound. I was introduced to screen-reading software called JAWS, which opened up an entirely new level of independence. Suddenly, I could read digital documents, write papers, and even browse the internet without needing someone to read everything to me. It felt like a door had swung open to a much bigger world.

It would take me until I was in my late 20s to fully realize how much this school and my parents taught me. Parkview is more than just a school for blind kids—it's a family. Some of the kids I knew there didn't have loving parents or supportive relatives. For them, the staff and teachers at the school were their family. They were the ones who showed up for them, not just in the classroom, but in life. They cheered for us when we succeeded, and they pushed us when we needed it. We used to joke that the school was like a prison, but deep down, we all knew it was a place that had our backs.

Over the years, people have asked me whether I would recommend sending their students to the school today. It's not an easy question to answer. Times have changed a lot, and so has the way the school operates. The classes are much smaller, which means more one-on-one instruction from teachers. The typical student is often years behind traditional students academically, which can be both a challenge and a benefit depending on their needs. At Parkview, you learn Braille and you use it every day. In a typical public school, you might only get Braille instruction once a week from a specialist who travels between schools. That daily repetition at Parkview is a game changer.

But technology, resources, and even society have evolved since my time there. Now, students have access to social media, visual rehabilitation therapists, and specialized training centers that can teach daily living skills. Assistive technology has advanced in ways we couldn't have imagined when I was a student—something I'll get into more later in this book. So my answer is always: it depends on the student. The right school is the one that will give them the most tools to live fully, and for some, that may still be Parkview.

Looking back, I realize my journey wasn't just about learning to navigate blindness—it was about learning to navigate life itself. Like a ship leaving the safety of the harbor, I was unsure of the waters ahead. I didn't know if the winds would carry me forward or push me back. But with the support of my parents, the dedication of my teachers at Parkview, and the lessons I learned in those years, I've found my own compass. Now, I sail forward, confident in my direction, anchored by the love and guidance that helped me set out on this course in the first place.

Take Away:

The detour is sometimes the destination. And sometimes you may need an awkward experience to make you do things differently.

If you'd told younger me that a detour could become the main road, I would've laughed. Back then, I believed life was supposed to be a straight line: point A to point B with no pit stops, no surprises, no awkward left turns. Everything was supposed to be predictable if you worked hard enough and stayed focused. But here's the thing about life—it doesn't consult you before rearranging the route. And the detour? It rarely looks appealing when you first take it. In fact, most of the time it looks inconvenient, messy, and a little humiliating.

When my vision started changing, I thought the only way to handle it was to keep pushing forward the way I always had. Same habits, same routines, same stubbornness. I didn't want to learn Braille. I didn't want to use a cane. I didn't want to stand out as "the blind kid." I wanted to keep my image, my comfort, my pride. But life had other plans, and let me tell you, pride doesn't get very far when you can't see the curb in front of you.

Some of my most important turning points didn't feel profound in the moment—they felt embarrassing, frustrating, even humiliating. Like the first time I tripped in front of a crowd, or the moment I realized I couldn't read the board no matter how close I sat. I wanted to hide from those moments, to erase them from memory. But they were the ones that finally nudged me toward change. Without them, I wouldn't have picked up a cane. Without the cane, I wouldn't have learned independence in a whole new way. Without that independence, I wouldn't have built the confidence to navigate spaces that once terrified me.

That's the thing about awkward experiences: they strip you of the option to keep pretending. They push you into action. They force you to ask, "What's actually going to help me here?" And once you stop resisting, you realize that what felt like a side road might actually be leading you exactly where you need to go. The road that seems like a detour often has the clearest view of what truly matters.

Looking back, I see those detours differently. They weren't punishments. They weren't proof that I was losing control of my life. They were invitations—to grow, to adapt, to learn that identity isn't tied to the tools you use. I had to let go of the picture-perfect route I'd drawn in my head so I could actually start living on the one that was real, even if it was bumpier, even if it took longer.

If you're in the middle of your own detour right now, here's what I'll tell you: stop fighting the road you're on just because it doesn't look like what you expected. Some paths are only visible once you walk them. Some lessons are only learned through discomfort. And sometimes the most awkward, uncomfortable moments are the very ones that turn you into someone you never imagined you could be.

So yeah—the detour is sometimes the destination. And if it takes a little awkwardness to push you in a new direction? Consider it the toll fee. Pay it, learn from it, and keep moving forward with your head high.

CHAPTER 4

A Town, A Life, A Journey Through Limitations

———◆———

While living in Muskogee, I continued to spend plenty of time with my friends at school, building on old friendships and forming new ones through church activities and other local opportunities. This period was about carving out a life that felt mine, in a town that was new but slowly becoming familiar. In addition to school, I took drum lessons, which became a meaningful way to engage with rhythm and sound, especially since sound was one of my strongest senses. Drumming allowed me to express emotions and energy in ways that words sometimes couldn't capture.

Alongside drumming, I also signed up for karate classes. Karate wasn't just about physical activity or learning to defend myself; it was about discipline, control, and self-confidence. Each session helped me build not only muscle memory but also trust in my own abilities, which was crucial when sight wasn't always reliable. On top of those, I found myself participating in several productions at the local theater. This was one of the more surprising parts of my life back then because, in both plays I was cast in, I played a 10-

year-old, even though I was actually 16 years old at the time. At the time, I found this quite strange—playing a child when I was nearly an adult. But looking back, it was one of those unexpected blessings that comes with having a youthful face. It meant I always looked younger than I was, which sometimes helped me blend into different social situations with less attention.

As you'll read throughout this book, I've never really had difficulty meeting new people. I tend to be open and approachable, though it sometimes takes me a little longer to truly get to know someone beneath the surface. One of the unique things about how I connect with people is that I recognize them mostly by their voices. After hearing someone speak a few times, I begin to associate their voice with their identity and presence. This method of recognition has been a constant in my life, a helpful tool for navigating social interactions. Most people tend to forget that I'm blind—probably about ninety-nine percent of the time. Even my parents and family sometimes forget in moments, which speaks to how much they treat me like anyone else. I honestly can't count the number of times someone has said, "I saw you at the event and waved," only to later remember with surprise, "Oh… we forgot you couldn't see me." It's a funny reminder that I'm often just treated as "Trey," rather than "the blind kid," which is exactly how I want it.

Of course, my blindness sometimes led to situations that were a bit tricky or funny, especially with friends who enjoyed teasing or pushing boundaries. For example, during a youth video adventure hunt, our group had to improvise playing an impromptu baseball game in a parking lot—only without using a real bat or ball. My friend and youth pastor came up with the idea to use my white cane as the bat and a roll of toilet paper as the ball. The image was hilarious, and while it might have been a bit reckless, it showed how our community could be creative and supportive all at once. On another occasion, some of my buddies tried to play the sympathy card with girls, hoping to get them to feel sorry for me because of my blindness. However, those attempts never lasted long because one of our lady friends quickly called them out, cutting through the nonsense. I also once had someone think I was faking being blind. I mean, if I was going to fake it, wouldn't I at least be better at it? Moments like that remind me how much misunderstanding still exists around blindness, but that's part of the challenge I've learned to navigate.

Summers were a different kind of freedom. When I wasn't away at camp, you could almost always find me at the lake or in the pool, soaking in the water and the sun. Water skiing became a favorite activity, though it took me several years to truly master it. I recall countless summers where I'd strap on the skis, start to rise up, and then fall halfway through the attempt. This cycle of falling and trying again repeated year after year. My stubborn determination eventually paid off. Once I finally got the hang of it, water skiing became one of my greatest joys. I even tried wakeboarding one day out of curiosity—it looked thrilling. Amazingly, I got up on my first try and was gliding smoothly over the water, but then I caught the edge of the board and slammed hard into the water, which felt like hitting concrete. After that rough introduction, I quickly retreated to my skis, deciding it was better to stick with what I knew for a while longer.

During this same period, I also began honing my public speaking skills. In middle school, my class participated in the state science fair. The competition placed a heavy emphasis on how well we presented our findings, not just the experiment itself. I ended up winning state in my division—and the overall competition too! Honestly, I think my teacher was more excited than I was. She was so proud that one of her students had won such a prestigious award that she celebrated wildly, leaving me to stand at the back of the auditorium after my speech. It was the moment I first realized how much I loved public speaking and sharing ideas. Ironically, most people wouldn't guess that I spent years in speech therapy as a child, working hard to strengthen the muscles in my mouth and improve my clarity. When I finally could speak clearly, I had a strong Southern accent, something I wasn't even aware of at the time. I quickly lost that accent when I went off to college, but sometimes it comes back when I spend long periods with family or get very tired.

Around this time, my friends—both in Comanche and Muskogee—were preparing to get their driver's licenses. This milestone felt like an emotional anchor for me. Until then, I hadn't really thought much about being blind as a limitation. But this was the first major obstacle that reminded me of what I couldn't do. I desperately wanted to jump in a car and drive somewhere—anywhere—just for the independence that driving represents. I still feel that longing sometimes, but I've learned to accept my situation, in part because of a conversation with my cousin. He helped me reframe how I saw my blindness. He said, "Trey, yeah, you can't drive—but think about it: your stress level is probably lower because you don't have to deal with idiots on the road. Plus, think about how much money you're saving by not having car payments or gas expenses." That change in perspective helped me more than he likely knew. Plus, with the rise of rideshare services, getting around by car is no longer limited to taxis or paratransit options, which is a huge relief.

I should also admit something: I've always had a knack for talking my mom into almost anything. One idea I thought would be really cool was to host a foreign exchange student in our home. After lots of convincing, she finally agreed, and we welcomed a young man around my age from Brazil into our family. Lucas became a great addition. Although we sometimes had disagreements and our own unique family dynamics, we always supported one another. Over time, he became more like a brother than just someone who lived with us for a semester. After he returned home, we kept in touch, sometimes using calling cards because, to the younger readers, we didn't always have WhatsApp or Facebook Messenger back then. Eventually, though, we lost contact for a while. Then one day, we reconnected on Facebook, and he visited us again during a college abroad program in the states. He's like a groundhog—he pops up once a year just to say "Feliz aniversário"—Happy Birthday.

As I kept moving forward with my life, I had no idea that one of my first true "valley seasons" was just ahead—a difficult time when faith, family, friends, and prayer would become more essential than ever before.

Take Away:

Your limitations are just plot twists — keep showing up.

Listen, life isn't a perfectly scripted movie where everything goes as planned. If you're expecting a neat narrative, a straight line from start to finish, I'm here to tell you—reality isn't interested in playing by those rules. Life is messy, unpredictable, and often uncomfortable. You're going to face moments that throw you off course, detours you didn't see coming, and limitations that seem like stop signs. But here's the truth: those limitations? They aren't the end of your story. They're just plot twists. And how you show up after those twists—how you respond, adapt, and push forward—that's what shapes your story's real meaning.

I know this because I've lived it. For most of my life, blindness was that plot twist I never asked for. It was something I saw as a wall—a barrier to the normal life I thought I was supposed to have. I tried to keep running straight ahead, pushing myself to fit the same mold as everyone else, stubbornly resisting the changes I needed to make.

Here's the thing: limitations show up in every life. Not always blindness, but in some form or another. It might be a health challenge, a loss, a failed dream, a relationship breaking down, or a new reality you never wanted to face. And those moments feel like derailments. Like your life is going off script and you're left stumbling in the dark, unsure what to do next. It's easy to get stuck there, to let the limitation define you, to see it as proof that you're somehow less than you hoped.

But what if, instead of being a dead end, your limitation is actually an invitation? An invitation to rewrite your story, not in the way you planned, but in a way that's just as rich and meaningful. What if your detours—awkward, frustrating, and unexpected as they are—are actually part of your unique path?

Those moments force us to face what's really going on. They strip away the option to pretend that everything's fine. Sometimes it takes falling flat on your face, tripping in front of everyone, or hearing someone question your truth to push you toward change. And while change is uncomfortable, it's also necessary. It's how you grow.

Keep in mind: limitations don't define your worth or your future. They don't take away your value or your ability to impact the world. They're simply parts of your plot—twists that make your story more real, more complex, and ultimately more compelling.

When I reflect on my time growing up in Muskogee, on the friendships I made, the drum lessons, karate classes, and theater productions I took part in, I realize how much I was learning to show up differently. I was learning resilience. I was learning creativity. I was learning that even if my body or my eyes didn't work the way I wanted, my spirit could still push me forward.

Water skiing was another example. I spent years falling, failing to stand up, crashing down mid-attempt. It was frustrating and humbling, but I kept trying. I was stubborn enough to not give up, even when it seemed impossible. And when I finally got the hang of it, the joy was unforgettable. That persistence, fueled by hope and determination, is the heart of showing up despite limitations.

And yes, I still carry around those moments when I feel the sting of what I can't do—like not being able to drive when all my friends were getting their licenses. That was a hard reminder of my limitations, a real emotional anchor that made me feel different. But thanks to perspective—sometimes offered by family, like my cousin's practical reminder about the perks of not driving—I learned to reframe those limitations. Instead of wallowing in what I lost, I began to see what I gained: less stress, financial savings, and the freedom that comes with rideshare and other services. It's a different kind of independence, but independence nonetheless.

The truth is, limitations don't just close doors; they open new ones. They challenge us to discover new strengths and new ways of living. It's not about pretending everything's perfect or better than it is. It's about showing up, imperfectly, every day, and doing what you can with what you have.

This mindset shift is essential because life will continue to throw challenges your way. It doesn't hand out scripts that fit all our expectations. It throws plot twists, detours, and unexpected guests into the mix. But you get to choose how you respond.

You can sit on the sidelines, wishing things were different, or you can get back in the game, learning to navigate the new rules. You can resist, or you can adapt. You can let limitations be the end of your story, or you can make them the catalyst for your next chapter.

And here's something I want you to hold on to: showing up isn't about big, dramatic moments every day. Sometimes it's the small things—getting out of bed, facing a difficult conversation, trying something new, or simply choosing to keep moving forward even when you're tired and frustrated. Those small acts of courage add up. They build momentum. They shape who you become.

Faith, for me, became a cornerstone in learning to keep showing up. It wasn't a magic fix, but it was a steadying force. It reminded me that my story wasn't just about me. That even when I felt stuck or sidelined, there was a greater plan unfolding. It gave me hope and strength to lean into the uncertainty.

If you're walking through your own valley season, your own tough chapter filled with limitations, setbacks, or pain, remember: this is not your end. It's a part of your journey. Your limitations are not your prison—they're your plot twists. And your willingness to keep showing up, to keep rewriting your story, is what will define your legacy.

So don't wait for perfect conditions, a clear path, or the absence of obstacles. Don't let the fear of failure or the sting of limitation keep you from living fully. Show up, keep showing up, and trust that each step, no matter how small or awkward, is moving you forward.

Because the best stories—the ones that resonate and inspire—aren't about flawless heroes who never falter. They're about real people who face their limitations head-on and keep going anyway.

Your limitations? They're just plot twists. Keep showing up.

CHAPTER 5

Seizures and Second Chances

It was the fall of my sophomore year of high school when life's first storm hit hard and without warning. My Papa passed away suddenly, and six weeks later, almost to the day, my cousin passed away too. These were my first encounters with profound loss, and I found myself navigating each in entirely different ways. Much later, I would come to understand that grief is deeply personal. No two experiences are alike, and the way we process sorrow evolves with each instance. At the time, though, I was simply overwhelmed, confused by the pain, unsure how to carry it.

Shortly after, I began experiencing some health issues. Initially, they seemed minor—nothing more than what could be corrected through a brief surgical procedure or a prescribed medication. But what happened next is something I only partially remember, and even now, recalling it stirs emotions I struggle to fully express.

It started as an ordinary evening. I had come home from school, eaten dinner, played with my dog, Boomer, and gone to bed. Boomer, as always, curled up on the body pillow at the foot of my bed. The radio played softly in the background, and I drifted off to sleep without a second thought.

The next thing I remember, I was awake—but in a fog. I was disoriented, walking aimlessly around my room, trying desperately to get out. Fear gripped me. I didn't know what was happening. I only knew one thing: I couldn't escape. I tried opening my bedroom door, but it was somehow locked from the inside. In a panicked attempt, I shattered a CD (for the younger readers, a CD is what music used to come on) and tried to slide it between the lock and the frame to force the door open. Nothing worked.

Then suddenly, my mom burst into the room. She found me attempting to crawl out of my bedroom window. I broke down into her arms, crying. She later told me that Boomer had been barking nonstop, which woke her up. That one act may have saved me. I still remember the song that was playing on the radio: "You're Gonna Miss This" by Trace Adkins. It would be years before I could listen to that song again without breaking down.

My mom immediately called the fire station in Oklahoma City to wake up my dad, who was working overnight. We were both terrified and completely in the dark. We had no clue what was happening.

Now, I know what you're probably thinking: "Trey, were you high? Were you drunk?" That was our first thought too—

and honestly, it would've been a far simpler explanation. But the truth was far more complicated—and far more terrifying.

After a series of medical tests and a few more unsettling episodes, we finally received an answer: I had suffered a seizure, the result of a tumor located in the front left lobe of my brain.

That diagnosis set in motion a whirlwind of medical procedures and travel between our home and M.D. Anderson Cancer Center in Houston. I underwent EEGs, MRIs, and a new test at the time called a MEGG test. I was placed on anti-seizure medications. Unfortunately, the medications failed to control the episodes.

An MEGG test is an MRI and EEG combined in one. I was taken into a small room and had electric probes placed on my head. Then, after the MRI portion was completed, I went into the EEG part, answering questions asked by the technician and trying to relax. I was told by my parents that one of the tests took so long because the machine shut off— the temperature got too warm for the machine to operate correctly.

The seizures continued—especially at night. Initially, they were classified as focal (or partial) seizures, but they soon escalated into full tonic-clonic seizures, more commonly known as grand mal.

The seizures began to consume my life. They left me anxious, isolated, and emotionally drained. My once-outgoing, cheerful personality grew dim. I no longer felt like myself, and eventually, I began to doubt whether I could continue with school. I remember telling my mom, "I don't think college is for me. I think I'll just stay home." Deep down, we all knew that wasn't my heart talking; it was the illness, the fear, the weight of uncertainty.

One particularly severe night, I had multiple seizures in rapid succession and was rushed to the hospital. Each time I had one of these episodes, the paramedics administered medication that essentially sedated me. It was a helpless cycle. My parents, desperate for answers, contacted my doctor in Houston. He told us to return immediately.

We packed the car and prepared to make the now-familiar trip to Houston. But that morning, something strange happened—something that would stick with us forever.

My mom, who worked in real estate around the Muskogee area, had a last-minute showing with a client. He was impatient and demanding. She told him she was about to leave town for her son's medical crisis, but the man insisted she show him the property. He was, she later learned, a physician. During the showing, he was cold and curt, and as he got into his car, he said something unexpected: "You know they can do surgery for your son." Then he got in his car and drove off.

We never saw or heard from him again. He didn't leave a card, a name, or any way to contact him. To this day, we don't know who he was. Maybe a doctor. Maybe an angel. But those words—uttered in passing—sparked a conversation with my doctors that changed my life.

In Houston, we spent hours discussing surgical options. After numerous consultations, I was referred to a highly specialized neurosurgeon who could perform cortical mapping—a cutting-edge technique designed to pinpoint the exact origin of my seizures in the brain. This wasn't a quick or simple process. It required a full week-long stay in the hospital, during which I was monitored continuously, 24 hours a day, 7 days a week. My head was wired up to an EEG machine, with electrodes carefully placed to track every flicker of electrical activity in my brain. Every twitch, every shift, every tiny movement I made was recorded meticulously. The experience was both physically exhausting and mentally overwhelming, but it was necessary to gain the precise information needed for surgery. After days of monitoring and data collection, the specialists finally identified the specific area responsible for triggering my seizures. It was a breakthrough moment. Six weeks later, armed with this critical knowledge, I was scheduled for a procedure that would change everything: awake brain surgery.

Yes—you read that correctly: awake.

On February 10, 2010, I checked into Hermann Memorial Hospital, ready to undergo a surgery that would last over nine hours. I remember bits and pieces of that day vividly. The operating room was a strange combination of clinical coldness and bizarre familiarity. The neurosurgeon made an effort to keep me calm and engaged throughout the procedure, cracking jokes to ease my nerves and keep me responsive. I wasn't just lying there passively; I was an active participant. At one point, they asked me to recite nursery rhymes aloud, and then to sing "Row, Row, Row Your Boat." I wasn't thrilled about singing during brain surgery, but I understood the importance—it helped them map the functional areas of my brain and avoid damaging critical language centers.

Then, something unexpected happened. In the middle of singing, the words suddenly vanished from my mind. I could feel my mouth moving, forming sounds, but I couldn't actually hear myself. For a terrifying moment, it felt like language itself had slipped away—that I'd lost my ability to communicate. And then, as suddenly as it had disappeared, the words returned, flooding back into my consciousness.

Even stranger was the moment when, with my skull open and my brain exposed, I spoke to my parents on the phone. I was literally mid-operation, talking with my family while surgeons worked around me. That surreal image—me on the phone during brain surgery—is something I still find hard to believe myself.

Tell me that's not wild.

When I finally returned home after the surgery, I never had another seizure again. Not one.

Recovery wasn't immediate. I couldn't simply pick up where I left off and jump back into school or life as normal. My body needed time to heal, and my mind needed even more. I was far from completely restored to my old self—but I was stable, and for the first time in many years, I truly felt like the storm had passed.

I finished my senior year with a new sense of hope. College started to feel possible again. But that journey—that chapter—deserves its own story.

This time in my life wasn't defined only by pain. There were moments of light, too. My faith sustained me. My family held me up. And an army of prayer warriors lifted me when I couldn't stand on my own.

And there was one last, unforgettable memory: Not long after returning home, our school received tickets to see Paul McCartney at a concert. I had no idea who he was at the time—but I do now. And for our senior class photo, I climbed up onto the brick wall outside the school, dressed in my cap and gown, smiling wide. I made it. The storms had come, but they haven't taken me yet. But like any captain, there is always another valley season.

Take Away:

Embrace the Storm — Find Light in Life's Darkest Valleys

Life's hardest trials often come unannounced, shaking the very ground beneath us. Loss, illness, fear — these storms can feel overwhelming, isolating, and utterly confusing. When they hit, it's like the rug has been pulled out from under your feet and you find yourself tumbling into a valley that feels impossibly deep and dark. And yet, it's precisely in these valleys — those moments and seasons of raw vulnerability — that we begin the slow, often painful process of healing and transformation.

The chapter you just read walks through one such valley, one that arrived suddenly and fiercely. The unexpected loss of loved ones, the emergence of a terrifying illness, the fear of the unknown — these are not just plot points in a story. They are lived realities that shake a person to their core. What makes these experiences so challenging is that they come without a rulebook, no roadmap, no guide on how to "get through" or even how to feel in the moment. You can't prepare for a storm like this because it demands your full presence, your rawest emotions, and a willingness to face the uncertain head-on.

What stands out most — and what I hope resonates with you — is the deeply personal nature of grief and healing. Grief is not a one-size-fits-all experience. It doesn't follow a linear timeline or a neat checklist of stages. Some days you may feel numb, other days you may be consumed with waves of sadness or anger. You might cry for hours, or you might not shed a tear at all. There is no "right way" to grieve, no perfect schedule, no deadline. Each person's journey through loss is unique, shaped by their relationship with what was lost, their inner strength, their support system, and even their faith or belief system.

Similarly, healing from trauma, illness, or any life-altering event unfolds on its own clock. You might think you should be "over it" by now, or that you're progressing too slowly. But the reality is that healing is often non-linear — it comes in fits and starts, advances and setbacks. You may feel like you're taking two steps forward and one step back, and that's okay. It's part of the process. Sometimes healing looks like acceptance, sometimes it looks like stubborn resilience, and sometimes it simply looks like getting out of bed and putting one foot in front of the other.

What this chapter beautifully illustrates is that even when life seems like a relentless storm, there is always light — sometimes faint, sometimes glaring — waiting to be found. The light might come from your faith, which can become a steady anchor in the wildest winds. It might come from family, whose love and presence provide a tether to hope when you're at risk of drifting away. It might come from community, from prayer warriors, from friends, or even from moments of unexpected kindness and grace.

One of the most powerful lessons here is that storms do not have to define us. They test us, yes. They can break us, if we let them. But they also have the capacity to shape us — to carve out new spaces of strength, clarity, and compassion. What you see in this chapter is a testimony to that truth: amid seizures, surgeries, and devastating loss, the narrator finds an unyielding spirit, the beginnings of hope, and a path toward reclaiming life.

There's something profoundly human about learning to embrace the storm — about accepting that some days will be dark, some moments unbearably heavy — but also about believing that light exists on the other side. That belief is what carries people through the valley seasons. It's what encourages them to keep fighting, keep praying, keep hoping, even when the way forward is unclear.

It's important to also acknowledge the role of grace and unexpected moments in the healing journey. Like the mysterious doctor who quietly gave a word of hope, or the neurosurgeon who used humor and music to guide a patient through awake brain surgery — these glimpses of light show us that even in the bleakest moments, human connection and kindness can spark courage and resilience.

If you find yourself in a valley right now — whether it's grief, illness, or another kind of deep struggle — I want to remind you that your feelings are valid and your pain is real. There's no shame in being scared or in needing help. You don't have to have all the answers or "be strong" all the time. Healing is messy and slow. But the act of showing up for yourself every day — even when you don't feel like it — is one of the bravest things you can do.

Allow yourself to grieve without judgment. Reach out for support, whether that's family, friends, faith communities, or professionals. And hold onto hope — even when it feels like a flicker. That flicker is a seed that can grow into something transformative.

Ultimately, this chapter reminds us that life's storms are part of the human experience, but they don't get the final say. The final say belongs to resilience, faith, love, and the quiet but powerful decision to keep moving forward — no matter how hard it gets.

Remember: embracing the storm doesn't mean you have to like the rain. It means learning to dance in it until the skies clear. It means understanding that valleys, as dark as they feel, are not the end of the story — they are chapters in a larger journey. And those chapters, painful as they may be, often contain the seeds of growth, wisdom, and renewed purpose.

So if you're navigating your own storm today, know that you're not alone. There is light ahead. There is hope. And there is a strength within you that will carry you through.

CHAPTER 6

Finding My Lane on Campus

Two weeks after graduating from Parkview, my parents—along with a few family friends—packed up everything we owned and moved our little family to Oklahoma City. It was a strange mix of excitement and uncertainty, the kind of change that feels like standing on the edge of a diving board, not quite sure how cold the water will be. When we arrived, we were met by my Granny, my aunts, and a handful of old friends who rallied around us, helping us settle into our new home.

Once again, I was in unfamiliar territory. But this time, there was no high school looming over me, no awkward freshman jitters, and—most importantly—no seizures threatening to disrupt my every move. Still, if you've followed my journey up to this point, you already know: staying settled has never been one of my strong suits. I'm the type who always seems to be adjusting to something new, even when I think I've found solid ground.

A few weeks after the move, my dad and I began walking the campus of the University of Central Oklahoma (UCO) in Edmond. That summer became a blur of campus tours—just the two of us weaving our way past brick buildings, grassy quads, and quiet study spots. We walked almost every inch of that place, trying to etch its layout into my brain before classes even started.

Then, seemingly out of nowhere, I got a phone call from a woman named Debi—a loud, eccentric, borderline-crazy woman (and I say "crazy" with nothing but affection). She asked if I needed help getting familiar with UCO. Before I could overthink it, Debi showed up at my parents' doorstep, ready to whisk me away for yet another campus tour. We walked the grounds again… and again… and again. Thanks to her persistence—and my parents' support—I ended up walking the campus one or two times a week, every week, until it felt almost second nature. That "crazy old lady" not only became a dear friend, but eventually, a coworker.

Now, you might be wondering how Debi earned her colorful reputation. During one of our walks, she warned me that in the first week of school, every Greek organization, club, and volunteer group would be lined up along Broncho Lake. "It'll be chaos," she said, with the tone of someone who'd seen it happen a hundred times. Me? I brushed it off. I told her I'd be fine. After all, I knew the campus layout like the back of my hand. In fact, I planned on rushing a fraternity, so I figured a big crowd would be an advantage.

Well… she was right.

Getting to my 9:00 a.m. class that first day was a breeze. But when I stepped outside at 10:00, it was like the entire student body had decided to descend on Broncho Lake at once. I was swallowed up in a sea of chatter, music, and movement, my sense of direction gone in seconds. If it hadn't been for a guy I'd met earlier in the week, I might've wandered in circles for hours. Even though I knew the student union pretty well, just walking in to grab a sandwich felt overwhelming with so many bodies pressing in around me. Another guy—also from that same fraternity—guided me through the food line without making it awkward.

By the end of the week, I'd run into several more members of that fraternity. The more I interacted with them, the clearer it became: Kappa Sigma was the one I needed to rush.

Now, I won't sugarcoat it—these guys were wild. Sometimes selfish, sometimes annoying, often ridiculous. But they were also fiercely loyal. They didn't tiptoe around me because of my disability. They teased me, gave me a hard time, and treated me like a brother in every way that mattered. And that was exactly what I'd been hoping to find. So to all my Kappa Sig brothers: A->B.

It's worth mentioning that my first day at UCO came almost exactly six months after brain surgery. I was still in recovery, still finding my footing—literally and figuratively. I was in a brand-new city, surrounded by total strangers, and the realization hit me hard: I was behind. Not just academically, but socially and mentally, too. I'd expected some of that, but expecting it and living it are two different things. Adjusting to college life while healing was an uphill climb.

I could've chosen to play it safe, stay tucked away in the dorms, and keep a low profile. But that's never been my style. I wanted the full college experience, bumps and all. My new roommate was someone I'd never met before, and while we didn't always see eye to eye, I look back now and feel nothing but gratitude. He was steady where I was uncertain, patient where I was naïve. In those early months, he was part of the reason I began learning how to exist in a world that wasn't built to bend around my needs.

Living blind in a sighted world meant I had to become my own advocate—and fast. There was no manual, no guide, just me figuring out how to get food from the cafeteria without looking completely lost, and how to find an open seat without bumping into half the room first. After a few awkward attempts on my own, people started to recognize me and step in when I needed it. They learned my rhythms; I learned theirs. In the process, I think I helped open a few eyes—showing that blind people can do almost everything sighted people do, we just go about it differently.

One of the earliest skills I had to master was the art of dodging, dipping, and weaving my way through campus obstacles—skateboarders flying past like human projectiles, low-hanging tree branches ready to smack me in the face, and people so glued to their phones they might as well have been walking blind themselves. On my very first day, I headed to the student union for a cup of coffee. Just as I was about to cross from the dorms to the main campus, the sprinklers kicked on without warning. Yep—got soaked. Not drenched enough for people to notice, but enough to make me start changing my route or picking up my pace in the mornings. My friends used to joke that I should wear a hidden camera to capture the looks people gave me when unexpected things like that happened. Apparently, it would've been comedy gold.

My fraternity brothers never held back—and thank God for that. One afternoon, we were sitting on a bench outside class when a few girls walked by. Out of habit more than anything, I turned my head to follow them. Without missing a beat, my friend smacked the back of my head and said, "Dude, knock it off." I asked him what he meant, and that's when he hit me with the truth bomb.

"How do you do it? Or are you faking?" he said. "Those girls were gorgeous, but when you tracked them with your head, they looked creeped out. You don't look blind, man. So, when you do that, they think you're just being a creep."

Point taken. I straightened up, faced forward, and decided maybe I'd just move my eyes next time instead. He smacked me again. "Don't do that either! Same thing. If you don't want to look like a creep, pretend to be busy—check your phone, work on your laptop—just stop tracking people like you're scanning for enemy movement."

That conversation stuck with me. Most people don't have the guts to say something like that, but that's exactly why I kept friends like him close. I've got a hundred stories like it. In a world that often hesitates to tell the truth—especially to someone with a disability—having people who will call you out is essential.

College wasn't always easy. I've always been fiercely independent, the type who hates asking for help unless there's absolutely no way around it. But I learned quickly: sometimes you need to ask, and sometimes you have to figure it out solo. One of the hardest emotional hurdles during that time was not being able to drive. I wanted to just grab the keys, get behind the wheel, and escape for a while—to explore, to clear my head, to feel that sense of control. Instead, I relied on friends. I know they didn't always feel like playing chauffeur, but I made it a point to chip in for gas or treat them to food whenever I could.

Academically, some classes felt like climbing a greased pole. I ended up hiring a fraternity brother—who later became one of my best friends—to read for me and help with tutoring. He had no problem telling me I was a terrible writer. Honestly, he wasn't wrong. I hated writing back then. Grammar? Forget it. His now-wife once told me I was an "elbow writer"—meaning my thoughts would fall off somewhere between my brain and the page. He also helped me survive math, which is especially brutal for blind students. Another friend pulled me through video editing classes that weren't compatible with my voiceover software. Without them, I doubt I would have made it through those semesters.

The friend who helped me through my video editing class eventually became one of my closest friends. We grew so tight that he ended up as my roommate for my final two semesters at UCO. Living together was a mix of late-night conversations, shared meals, and the kind of unspoken understanding that comes from having each other's backs. I stood beside him on his wedding day, watching him start his next chapter, and over the years, we've stayed connected. Every so often, I'd meet up with him, his wife, and later their two daughters, just to catch up and laugh about old stories that never seemed to get old.

During my time at UCO, I crossed paths with so many people—classmates, professors, fraternity brothers, musicians, and friends of friends—many of whom I still keep in touch with to this day. Each one of them shaped that season of my life in some way, whether through a single moment of kindness or years of steady friendship. That chapter of my life wasn't perfect, but it was one of the best. Andy Bernard from The Office said it perfectly:

"I wish there was a way to know you're in the good old days before you've actually left them."

Looking back, I know I was living those "good old days" without realizing it.

As I made my way through college, I began to feel more and more like myself. But if I'm being honest, I didn't truly feel whole until after my final semester. Somewhere along the way, I read that after brain surgery or trauma, it can take up to five years for someone to fully recover—not just physically, but mentally and emotionally too. To truly come back to themselves. For me, that rang true. It wasn't an overnight shift. It was slow, almost imperceptible, but looking back, I can see the steps I took toward becoming myself again.

I started out at UCO as a Mass Communication major, but—like most students—I found my plans shifting pretty quickly. Back in high school, a guy from my church had been accepted into UCO's Academy of Contemporary Music (ACM). He told me about a new Music Business program launching there, and the idea lodged in my mind. That program officially began during my freshman year. By my second semester, I decided to go for it—and I got in.

The Music Business department at ACM was unlike anything else on campus. It blended the structure of traditional academics with a creative, music-focused approach that made every class feel relevant and alive. In Composition I, we didn't write analytical essays on novels—we wrote them on songs. Even the business courses were tailored to the music industry, pulling us into real-world scenarios and case studies. At first, I thought I wanted to be an A&R rep, scouting and signing new talent. But somewhere along the way, I discovered my true love: songwriting. More specifically, I loved the matchmaking aspect of music publishing—pairing the right song with the right voice.

I became obsessed with the craft. I studied lyrics like they were poetry, listened to the subtle choices songwriters made, and imagined which artists could turn those words into something unforgettable. My plan was clear: gain experience in Oklahoma City, then head to Nashville to work with some popular songwriters.

ACM felt like home. It was the kind of place where you'd walk into the lounge and hear someone softly strumming a guitar, or pass a drummer in the hallway tapping out a rhythm on their knees. Music was in the air—literally. Every week, I discovered new artists, and my playlists grew until they felt like soundtracks to entire seasons of my life. Around that time, Spotify was just beginning to take off, and everyone at ACM could sense it was going to change the music industry forever.

On December 12, 2015, I walked across the stage and graduated from the University of Central Oklahoma with a degree in Music Business. I had completed my education, built friendships that felt like family, and soaked in every note of those years. At the time, I was certain I knew exactly where I was headed next.

Take Away:

You can't control when the sprinklers soak you or when life throws a crowd in your path — but you can control showing up, asking for help, and pretending to be busy so you don't look like a creep. That's how you win college and life. Also, remember to get a few good friends to be honest with you.

Here's the thing nobody tells you before you leave home: most of the things you'll remember about college will have nothing to do with classrooms, grades, or whatever is printed on your degree. They'll be about the tiny, ridiculous, awkward, human moments that happen in between. The way the sprinklers somehow always turn on when you're passing the one patch of grass you actually needed to cross. The crowd that seems to form exactly in front of you when you're in a hurry, moving at the speed of a glacier. That weird panic decision to whip out your phone and pretend you're replying to an urgent message, just so you don't look like some random person standing there with no purpose in life.

That's the real stuff. And — surprise — that's also where the lessons are hiding.

You can't control sprinklers. Not in life, and not on campus. You can't predict when someone's going to hit you with news that turns your week upside down. You can't tell in advance which people are going to ghost you after one semester, or which ones will still be checking on you ten years later. Life is just this endless, unpredictable series of "sprinkler moments" — small, inconvenient, sometimes comical disruptions that test your patience and your ability to adapt.

College taught me that those moments aren't just obstacles; they're opportunities to prove to yourself you can roll with it. You can dodge. You can laugh. You can keep walking through the mist like you planned it, because sometimes style points are the only points, you'll get.

And then there's the crowd factor. Oh, the crowd factor.

If you ever want to know how patient you really are, try getting somewhere on time when the only path forward is blocked by a wall of people who have apparently decided to walk in slow motion, three across, while having the deepest conversation of their lives. You'll discover, in those minutes, the fragile line between being a civilized human and turning into the main character of your own disaster movie.

In life, you will always encounter "crowds" — sometimes literal, sometimes emotional, sometimes even professional. People and situations that slow you down, take up space you thought was yours, and move at a speed that drives you insane. You can't bulldoze through without consequences, and you can't always politely wait for them to part. The trick is learning to navigate around them without losing your cool.

And yes, sometimes that navigation looks like pretending to be busy. Pulling out your phone so you don't look like the lone awkward soul standing on the fringe of a social moment you weren't invited into. Here's the truth: that's not just a survival tactic; it's a skill. The world rewards people who can act like they belong, even when they feel like they don't. That's the difference between going home early and meeting someone who changes your life just because you lingered another five minutes.

But the most important piece of winning college — and life — is this: show up.

Show up to the awkward events. Show up even when you don't feel like you have the right clothes, the right words, or the right mood. Half of life is just about being in the room when the good thing happens. The opportunity you want might be sitting there at the edge of the party you almost skipped, or hidden in a conversation that starts with "Hey, do you mind if I sit here?"

Showing up is also about asking for help. No one wins solo — not in college, and definitely not in the chaos of adult life. I used to think asking for help was a sign of weakness, like it made you look unprepared or incapable. Turns out, it's the opposite. The most capable people I know are the ones who know who to call, where to go, and what to say when they need support.

Here's the kicker, though: you need the right people in your corner.

Find friends who will be honest with you, not just nice to you. The kind who will tell you if you've got spinach in your teeth, if you're about to make a truly regrettable life choice, or if you're settling for less than you deserve. Honest friends are rare, because honesty costs effort and sometimes risks the friendship itself. But when you find them, you hold on — because they'll save you from mistakes you didn't even know you were making.

The truth is, "winning" life doesn't look like the movies. It's not about becoming the most popular, the most accomplished, or the most photogenic. It's about learning how to deal with the unpredictable in a way that leaves you intact — or better yet, a little wiser and a little funnier for having survived it.

When the sprinklers come on, you either run through them laughing or you find another route. When the crowd slows you down, you adjust your pace or you find a side path. When you feel like the weird outsider, you fake confidence until it feels real. When life knocks you flat, you get up and ask for help. And when someone loves you enough to be honest, you listen — even if it stings.

In the end, college doesn't really prepare you for life. Life is college, just without the tuition and the syllabus. Every day you're tested, graded in ways you'll never see, and given assignments you didn't sign up for. But the lessons — the real, useful, soul-deep ones — are free.

So no, you can't control when you get soaked or blocked or left standing alone. But you can control whether you keep showing up, whether you keep learning, and whether you keep finding ways to laugh at the chaos. That's not just how you win college — that's how you win life.

CHAPTER 7

The Hollow Places

I had finally graduated and was officially on the job hunt. Unlike many of my classmates, I hadn't made the rounds at job fairs during my senior year. I wasn't scatter-shooting my résumé to dozens of companies because I thought I had a clear, God-given plan: to work in the corporate offices of a local church. It felt safe. Familiar. Purpose-driven. In my mind, I was just waiting for the formality of the interview before I would step into my neatly envisioned future. Instead, one terrible interview later, that door didn't just close—it slammed, locked, and bolted shut. I left feeling stunned, not just because I didn't get the job, but because it made me question whether I'd heard God right at all. At the time, I was convinced He had called me into ministry. Looking back now, I can see that He was steering me elsewhere—down paths I would never have chosen, through seasons I would have gladly skipped.

Even after that, I still nursed a lifelong dream: to work in the music industry. But living in Oklahoma in the mid-2010s was like trying to be a deep-sea diver in the middle of a desert—wrong location, wrong environment. Opportunities were miles away, in cities I couldn't afford to move to, so I pivoted. I decided to take whatever job I could find, even if it had nothing to do with my passions. That decision became the opening chapter in what I now call my five-year valley season.

The valley was not dramatic—it was slow, grinding, and heavy. Day after day, I wrestled with depression and the creeping sense that I had somehow missed my one shot. Hope felt like something other people had the luxury of holding onto, while I was stuck adrift—like a ship lost at sea, searching for a shore that never came into view.

I had big dreams, but not a single door seemed willing to open. Years later, I came across a song by Dave Barnes called Chasing Dreams, and it stopped me in my tracks. In it, he sings about watching all of his friends' lives take off while his own plans keep falling apart. One line in particular— "How about a hint at how the ending will go"—felt like it had been written for me. I didn't need the entire roadmap back then. I wasn't asking for step-by-step instructions. I just wanted a small sign, some divine whisper that my story wasn't going to stay stuck in the middle forever.

During those years, I sat in front of so many interview panels that the routine almost became muscle memory—shake hands, smile, answer the usual questions, try to make a connection. But more often than not, it ended with some variation of the same line: "You don't have enough experience." Sometimes they said it gently, as though softening the blow would make the sting any less sharp. Other times, it came blunt and unvarnished, the kind of statement that left no room for doubt about their decision. Either way, I left with the same outcome—another "no" to add to the growing pile.

Not long ago, I saw a film about a man with a disability searching for a job and slamming into wall after wall. I thought I was just going to watch a story, but instead it hit like a punch to the gut. Scene after scene brought back my own memories in such vivid detail that my stomach actually tightened. I knew that weight in the chest, that knot in the throat, the gnawing temptation to throw in the towel. And yet, watching him also reminded me of something I knew deep down about myself: no matter how bad it got, quitting just wasn't in my nature. I could be tired, discouraged, and worn thin—but I would still keep trying.

At one point, I even took another internship at the same church where I had once hoped to work full-time. By then, I already knew a staff position wasn't going to materialize, but I went through with it anyway, partly out of a sense of commitment and partly because I wasn't sure what else to do. Unfortunately, the experience turned sour. It wasn't a single dramatic event—just a slow build of small frustrations and disappointments. By the time it ended, I'd made up my mind to leave that church completely. I'm still friends with some of the people there, but in hindsight, I can see that God wasn't merely nudging me; He was steering me firmly and unmistakably in another direction.

One interview from that period is still etched in my mind. It was with a local record label, and at first, everything seemed fine. We talked about music, about the role, about my skills. Then my blindness came up—not as a big revelation, just in the flow of conversation—and I watched their interest drain away in real time. Their smiles stayed, but the energy shifted. By the end, I knew I wasn't getting the job. At the time, it felt like yet another door slammed shut. But a month later, the FBI shut the whole place down. That rejection, it turned out, had been a gift in disguise.

Looking for a job right out of college is hard for anyone, but I had grown up believing the old formula: go to college, get your degree, and you'll get a good job. I carried that belief all the way to graduation, only to discover it wasn't the whole truth. A degree opened some doors, but experience was the real currency employers valued—and that was exactly what I didn't have. And whether they admitted it or not, my blindness was often another unspoken factor in the equation.

That led to one of the trickiest questions I faced during the job hunt: should I mention my disability up front or keep it off my résumé? Disclosing too soon sometimes felt like handing them a reason to reject me before we even met. Waiting until the interview meant risking that uncomfortable moment when the atmosphere in the room shifted, like it had at the record label. Neither choice felt safe. Still, I kept applying—sometimes sending out a whole stack of applications in a day, sometimes just one if that was all the mental energy I could manage.

Friends and family—my parents especially—suggested I consider a master's degree, perhaps in disability services. They weren't trying to box me in; they just wanted me to have a steady path. But I resisted. I didn't want to live in the "Blindness Box," where every step I took was expected to revolve around that one aspect of who I was. My ambitions reached beyond that label, and if that made my road harder, so be it.

By then, I wasn't just unemployed—I was also back living with my parents. I love them, and I'm grateful for everything they've done for me, but after years of living independently at college, it was an adjustment I didn't enjoy. Some of my friends were also living at home, but they had jobs, cars, and their own money. I had almost nothing. Relying on others for rides, for expenses, for practically everything—it ate away at my independence. I often felt like a ship in open water during a storm, waves pounding from every side, and no sight of land to aim for.

Then, at last, a door cracked open. A job in Tulsa—call center work, selling newspaper subscriptions for BH Media Group. Evenings, five days a week. Telemarketing wasn't my dream job, but it was a job. After so many rejections, that was enough to make me genuinely grateful.

During those months, I often repeated a line from a popular TV show describing selling paper as "utterly miserable." It became a running joke to myself, a way to survive the grind. Sometimes it made me laugh for real; other times, it was more of a grim smile through clenched teeth. But even on the hardest days, humor kept me afloat when little else did.

Take Away:

Life's "doors" don't always swing open the way we picture in our heads. We imagine some grand, cinematic entrance—the kind with dramatic lighting, a round of applause, and maybe a conveniently timed background song. Instead, real life tends to be more awkward. Sometimes the doors don't just close quietly; they slam. And not the polite kind of slam, either. I'm talking about the kind that rattles the walls and leaves you staring at the wood grain thinking, *Wow… was that personal?*

But here's the thing no one tells you: a slammed door is not the end. It's just a loud signal that you're not going that way—at least not today, not through that entrance. When one door slams, don't stand there frozen, replaying the moment, imagining all the reasons it happened. That's how you end up stuck in your own head, wondering if you should've worn a better outfit or spoken up more in class or smiled less in that interview so they didn't think you were desperate. None of that overthinking reopens the door.

What does? Knocking on the next one. Even if that next door doesn't look like much. Even if the only thing behind it is a job selling newspapers, tutoring kids, or doing the most random internship you never pictured for yourself. The point isn't that the new door is perfect—it's that you're moving forward. You're staying in motion. You're building muscle memory for persistence, because persistence is like Wi-Fi: the more you keep trying to connect, the more likely you are to get a signal.

I thought I knew exactly which door I was supposed to walk through after college. It was labeled neatly in my head: corporate ministry job at my local church. Safe. Familiar. Purposeful. I hadn't attended many job fairs during my senior year because I was convinced this was the plan. I didn't need to scatter résumés like birdseed. I had my door picked out, and I was ready to walk through it.

Then came the interview. The one that left me sitting in the car afterward, staring at the dashboard, wondering how quickly hope had turned into humiliation. It wasn't just that I didn't get the job—it was that I knew, the moment I walked out, that door had slammed shut. Not ajar. Not "maybe later." Slammed. Bolted.

At the time, I told myself God must be redirecting me, but deep down I wasn't convinced. I believed He was calling me to ministry, so why wasn't He making a way? Looking back, I can see what I couldn't see then—God had other paths in mind, paths I would never have chosen on my own.

I still had a dream tucked in my back pocket: working in the music industry. But living in Oklahoma in the mid-2010s wasn't exactly a front-row seat to opportunity. I didn't have the money or connections to pack up and move to Nashville or Los Angeles. So, I pivoted. I applied anywhere and everywhere—coffee shops, retail stores, office jobs. That decision marked the start of what I now call my five-year valley season.

The valley wasn't dramatic. It was quiet, grinding, and relentless. I sent out applications like messages in bottles, never knowing if they'd wash up on the right desk or just drift away unseen. With each "We've decided to move forward with other candidates," hope chipped away a little more. The worst part wasn't the big rejections—it was the slow erosion of confidence. The whispered story in my head began to sound believable: Maybe you're just not good enough.

Not all closed doors are as dramatic as my corporate ministry one. Some, like the record label interview I once had, are quieter but just as final. I thought it was my chance—until my blindness came up in conversation and the tone shifted.

The "no" was unspoken but unmistakable. Weeks later, the FBI shut the company down. What had felt like another personal rejection turned out to be protection. I'd been kept from boarding a sinking ship.

Of course, most slammed doors don't come with an obvious silver lining. More often, they just leave you with empty hands and unanswered questions. I lost count of the interviews where the feedback was some version of "You don't have enough experience." Sometimes it was delivered kindly. Other times, bluntly enough to sting. Either way, I walked away with another "no" and no clue what to try next.

Here's where persistence comes in—not the glamorous, motivational-poster kind, but the stubborn, exhausted, just-one-more-email kind. Even when my hope was running on fumes, I kept sending applications. Some days it was ten, other days only one, but I kept showing up. I learned that persistence isn't about never feeling discouraged—it's about knocking on the next door anyway.

Eventually, that persistence led me to Tulsa, to a job in a call center selling newspaper subscriptions. It was the kind of role sitcoms make fun of—the headset, the script, the endless rejections from people hanging up mid-sentence. It didn't move me any closer to my dream. But it was a paycheck. It was independence. And after years of slamming into locked doors, even a small, creaky one that opened into a telemarketing cubicle felt like progress.

Here's the strange truth: the jobs, relationships, and opportunities you think will define you often aren't the ones that do. More often, it's the ones you take because you can't afford not to. The ones that humble you. The ones that teach you to find humor in misery, to cling to grit when motivation runs dry, to keep knocking even when you've lost count of how many doors have stayed shut.

The trick is not letting those slammed doors define your worth. They're not always about you. Sometimes the timing is wrong. Sometimes the fit is wrong. And sometimes—just like with that record label—the building on the other side is on fire and you just don't know it yet.

That's why you can't stay planted in front of a closed door, demanding an explanation. You knock on the next one. And if that one doesn't open? You knock again. You knock at the ones that don't seem to fit your path. You knock until your knuckles are sore, until the hallway feels endless, until you finally hear the hinges move. Even the smallest opening can lead somewhere you need to be before you can get to where you want to be.

While you're knocking, keep people around you who tell you the truth. The friends who will warn you when you're chasing a dead end—or remind you when you're selling yourself short. The ones who will nudge you toward the next door when you've lost the energy to move on your own.

In the end, my valley season didn't break me, even though it came close. It stretched me. It stripped away some illusions. It taught me that the goal isn't to find the perfect door—it's to keep showing up in the hallway, ready to walk through the right one when it finally cracks open.

Life's "doors" don't always swing open the way we want; sometimes they slam so hard you feel the wind on your face. When that happens, don't waste your days staring at the wood grain, wondering what went wrong. Start knocking on the next one, even if it opens into a place you'd never have chosen on your own. You never know—your so-called "newspaper-selling season" might just be the step that makes the real door visible.

CHAPTER 8

The Unexpected Friendship

While living in Tulsa, I had the opportunity to speak at a fundraising luncheon for an organization that employed people with disabilities. This wasn't just any random event to me. I had attended many of their camps growing up, and they were the very same organization responsible for launching the call center at BH Media Group, a place where blind employees like me could work and thrive. In a way, it felt like I had come full circle—standing on their stage as living proof of the seeds they had planted years ago.

That afternoon, I stood in front of a crowd of about 500 people, delivering a memorized speech. Five hundred faces, five hundred sets of eyes on me, waiting to hear my story. It was one of my first official speaking gigs, and—just to prove it wasn't a fluke—I did it again six months later in Oklahoma City. Looking back now, I realize how much those moments prepared me for everything that came after, but at the time, I was just trying to remember my lines and not trip over the podium.

After my speech in Oklahoma City, something happened that I'll never forget. A woman approached me as the crowd began to thin. She introduced herself as a CEO—someone whose world was far removed from mine at the call center. She asked, "Have you ever had professional speech training?"

I shook my head and said, "No."

She smiled, locked eyes with me, and said, "You just gave a stellar speech." That simple sentence landed in my chest and stayed there. Not because I'd never been complimented before, but because it came from someone who knew what excellence looked like. Someone who didn't owe me encouragement, but gave it freely.

From that day on, she became more than a passing acquaintance. She became a friend. We had dinner a few times, swapping stories about life and work. She introduced me to numerous executives and CEOs, hoping to help me move beyond the call center grind. None of those connections landed me a job—but in the end, that wasn't really the point. Her presence in my life was a gift in itself. At a time when hope was in short supply, she reminded me it still existed. She encouraged me to keep honing my speaking skills, to keep telling my story even when I didn't feel like it mattered. And she was right—it did matter. It still does.

During my time in Tulsa, two other major things came into my life.

The first was my love for coffee shops. I'd always liked coffee, but my relationship with it was casual—usually at home, brewed in a simple machine, or picked up from big-name chains. But Tulsa opened my eyes to the charm of local cafés and the artistry behind a truly great cup of coffee. I discovered single-origin beans, hand-poured brews, and baristas who treated coffee like an Olympic sport. These places became my refuge—somewhere to sit, think, and be part of the hum of life without feeling like I was on the outside looking in. I've never been much of a beer drinker, but coffee? Coffee became my thing.

The second—and far more life-changing—was Shatner, my guide dog. Or as I lovingly call him, Shat.

Now, when I say "life-changing," I don't mean in the casual way people sometimes throw that phrase around, like when they find a new show to binge or discover a brand of ice cream that speaks to their soul. I mean in the literal, every-waking-moment sense of the word. Shatner didn't just give me mobility; he gave me a freedom I didn't even realize had been missing from my life. Before him, I moved through the world cautiously, counting steps, memorizing layouts, and depending on others in ways I had learned to normalize. With him, I moved differently—more fluid, more confident, less like I was calculating my every move and more like I was simply living.

I spent a month in New York that January training with him. That month was like a crash course in a new language—one made of leash signals, verbal commands, body cues, and mutual trust. From the moment we met, it was love at first snack. He leaned into me with this quiet assurance that said, "Don't worry, I've got you," though I didn't yet know if I could believe it. At first, I wasn't entirely sure if I'd enjoy working with a guide dog. It's a big responsibility—feeding, grooming, bonding, communicating. There are rules to follow and a constant awareness that you are caring for a living, breathing partner who depends on you as much as you depend on them.

But as the days passed, something shifted. We began moving through crowds like wind through trees, slipping past obstacles with a rhythm that felt instinctive. His paws seemed to know where my feet were going before I did. We became unstoppable, not because nothing could get in our way, but because together we could face whatever did.

Trust—now that's a big word for me. Not just with Shatner, but with people in general. Being blind means, I don't see the world the way others do. I have to rely on more than my instincts; I have to trust the people guiding me, the strangers helping me find a seat, the drivers taking me somewhere I can't verify on my own. Trust isn't optional; it's survival. And for someone like me, that kind of trust isn't handed out easily. It's earned, step by step, moment by moment.

And Shatner? He earned my trust faster than most humans ever have.

Let me tell you about this wild, beautiful creature—nicknamed "The Beast" by a friend who saw him in full playful mode. Shatner is a yellow English Lab with a pale pink nose and a coat so bright it's almost white, like someone took the word "golden" out of "golden retriever" and replaced it with "sunlight on fresh snow." When he's wearing his harness, he's the definition of professionalism—focused, attentive, and so alert he could probably tell you how many people in the room just shifted in their seats.

But the second that harness comes off, the professional disappears and the goofball takes over. He'll rocket around the house like a toddler after a sugar rush, skidding into furniture and bouncing back without missing a beat. He brings me toys—not just to throw, but to parade around like prized trophies—and if I don't acknowledge them, I get "the look." Then, just as quickly, he'll collapse into the world's most dramatic nap, limbs sprawled like he's auditioning for a role in some canine soap opera.

Food, of course, is his greatest weakness. I'm convinced he would sell state secrets for a single biscuit. And those big, pitiful eyes? They've fooled more than a few strangers into thinking he's been mistreated. I can't count how many times someone has bent down to give him sympathy scratches while giving me that unspoken "How could you?" look. Let me assure you—he is not deprived. If anything, he's a bit of a diva.

Take mornings, for example. Shatner hated waking up early with a passion that rivaled any teenager. The only thing that got him moving before sunrise was breakfast, and even then, he would grumble his way through the motions before slinking back to bed until 11 a.m., like some canine retiree who had earned the right to sleep in.

And the looks... oh, the looks. Shatner could communicate entire monologues with just one tilt of his head or shift of his ears. There's the "I hate you" look, the "You're interrupting my nap" look, the "Are you seriously eating that without me?" look, and my personal favorite, the "Fine, I'll forgive you, but only if you scratch behind my ears for the next twenty minutes" look. He is, and always has been, a little bit bonkers—but I wouldn't have survived Tulsa without him.

When I first got him, a friend who also had a guide dog told me something I've never forgotten: "Having a guide dog is like building a relationship with someone who knows you better than you know yourself. You are not two separate beings—you are one." At the time, I nodded politely, thinking it was a nice sentiment but maybe a touch exaggerated. Now I know they were absolutely right.

Over time, we learned to anticipate each other's moves, moods, and even hesitations. I could feel when he was about to pause or change direction before he actually did it. He seemed to sense when my energy was fading and adjusted his pace without a word from me. We weren't just navigating sidewalks together—we were navigating life.

Shatner taught me more than mobility. He taught me about partnership in its purest form—two beings working together, not because they have to, but because they trust each other completely. He taught me about trust without reservation, about leaning into the certainty that someone has your back even when you can't see what's ahead. And maybe most importantly, he taught me that sometimes the greatest gifts aren't the ones you earn through effort or ambition. They're the ones you're given unexpectedly, ready or not, that arrive just when you need them most.

Take Away:

Progress often starts with humble steps, and persistence opens new doors. Just keep walking and knocking on every door you can.

Sometimes those "doors" aren't the ones you were hoping to open, and sometimes they don't even look like doors at first. In Tulsa, my steps forward didn't arrive in the form of a dream job, a breakthrough career opportunity, or a neatly packaged success story. They came through a string of small, human moments—moments that at first seemed ordinary, but together began to shape the direction of my life.

One of the earliest of those moments was the speaking engagement at the fundraising luncheon. On the surface, it was just a short speech to a room full of people. But the room wasn't random—it was filled with faces connected to the very organization that had once invested in me. Years earlier, they'd been the ones running the camps I attended. They'd been the ones who launched the BH Media Group call center where people like me could work with dignity. I wasn't just another guest speaker; I was living proof that their efforts had mattered.

That day, I stood before 500 people, trying to keep my lines straight and my nerves steady. There was no grand promise that this speech would "change everything." But it was a step. A step toward finding my voice. A step toward believing my story had value to someone other than me. And when I got the chance to do it again in Oklahoma City, six months later, I took it—not because the first one had launched me into fame, but because persistence often means showing up for the second, third, and tenth opportunities before anything really shifts.

And then, one of those subtle shifts happened. After the Oklahoma City speech, the crowd began to thin, and a woman approached me. She was a CEO, a leader in her own right, far removed from my call center grind. She didn't owe me her time, but she gave it. She asked if I'd ever had professional speech training. I hadn't. She smiled and told me I'd just given a stellar speech. Those words landed differently because they came from someone who knew what excellence looked like.

It didn't get me a job. It didn't send me leaping into some new career field overnight. But it opened a door—a human door, one made of connection, encouragement, and genuine belief. We kept in touch. We had dinners, shared stories, and she introduced me to other leaders. None of those introductions landed a job either. But looking back, I can see the greater gift: she reminded me that my voice mattered and that I should keep honing it, even when no immediate payoff was in sight.

That's the thing about knocking on doors—you don't always know which one will open, and sometimes the ones that do open aren't the ones you expected. But each knock builds your resilience. Each knock teaches you to keep showing up.

Tulsa also gave me other gifts that weren't wrapped in career labels. One was the discovery of coffee shops—not just any coffee shops, but local cafés where the aroma hit you like a warm handshake and where the baristas treated coffee as though it were an Olympic sport. I'd always enjoyed coffee, but this was different. This was community in a cup. I found places where I could sit for hours, thinking, writing, or just listening to the hum of life around me. Those coffee shops became my little sanctuaries, places where I wasn't defined by what I was or wasn't accomplishing professionally.

And then there was Shatner.

Shatner was more than a guide dog; he was a turning point in my independence. Before him, my mobility had limits I didn't fully acknowledge. Training in New York for a month to work with him was an entirely new challenge—full of feeding schedules, grooming routines, and a crash course in mutual trust. In the beginning, I wasn't sure if I could handle the responsibility. But step by step, we learned each other's rhythms.

When he wore his harness, Shatner was all business—navigating crowds with precision, guiding me through spaces with a confidence that made me feel like we could walk straight through the middle of Times Square without missing a beat. But when the harness came off, the professional vanished, and the goofball emerged. He zoomed around like a sugar-high toddler, brought me toys, and flopped into exaggerated naps. His personality was as big as his loyalty.

He taught me trust in a way few people could. Being blind means trust is not optional—it's a matter of daily survival. With Shatner, I learned to lean into that trust without hesitation. We weren't just moving through sidewalks together; we were moving through life.

He had his quirks. He hated early mornings, would happily sleep until 11 a.m., and could guilt anyone with a single tilt of his head. He was dramatic, food-motivated, and a little bit of a diva. But he was also my partner—someone who knew my steps before I took them. A friend once told me that having a guide dog is like building a relationship with someone who knows you better than you know yourself. They were right.

The truth is, not one of these experiences—the speeches, the friendship with the CEO, the coffee shop refuge, or the bond with Shatner—looked like a big break from the outside. None of them instantly "solved" my professional challenges or erased the uncertainties in my life. But they were all steps forward, and sometimes that's how progress is made: quietly, steadily, one humble step at a time.

We're often taught to look for the moment when everything changes—the big door swinging wide. But life isn't always that cinematic. More often, it's a series of smaller doors that creak open just enough for you to slip through, and sometimes those doors aren't even about career advancement. Sometimes they're about building resilience, expanding your circle, discovering a place you feel at home, or learning to trust in ways you never have before.

Persistence isn't glamorous. It's not always rewarded immediately. But persistence shapes you. It's what keeps you walking to the next door, even after the last one slammed shut. It's what helps you recognize opportunity when it arrives in unexpected packaging—like a conversation after a speech, a cup of coffee in a quiet café, or a yellow English Lab with a pale pink nose.

If there's one lesson Tulsa taught me, it's that the forward motion you're looking for doesn't always come through the path you expect. It can arrive through people who believe in you without an agenda. It can arrive in places that give you peace without demanding productivity. And it can arrive in partnerships—human or canine—that expand your freedom and trust in ways you didn't even know you needed.

So, keep walking. Keep knocking. Not every door will open. Not every knock will be answered. But along the way, you might find something—or someone—that makes the journey worth continuing. Sometimes the most important doors aren't the ones that change your job title; they're the ones that change you.

CHAPTER 9

The Valley Season

The winter of 2019 tested me in ways I had not anticipated. I found myself standing at a crossroads, holding two job offers in my hands, each pulling my heart in completely opposite directions. One would allow me to remain in Tulsa, a city I had grown to love with a depth I hadn't known was possible. Tulsa had become more than just a place to live; it was a city that had slowly wrapped itself around me like a warm coat on a bitterly cold night. I had found a rhythm there, a sense of belonging that was rare and precious. The other offer pointed me back toward Oklahoma City, the place where my roots still ran deep. Most of my family, old friends, and familiar connections remained there, and with the job offer came the possibility of being closer to friends and family.

I didn't make the decision lightly. For weeks, I carried the weight of it in prayer. Every morning before sunrise, I would wake, read scripture, and plead with God for clarity. My faithful circle of prayer warriors stood with me, lifting my name in prayer as if it were their own burden. They encouraged me to listen for the whisper of God's voice, to trust His timing, even when the path was clouded in uncertainty. The Tulsa position looked appealing on the surface: a better salary than what I had been making at the call center, with the promise of stability. Yet there was also a sobering catch—it was located in one of the most impoverished areas of the city. The work would be emotionally taxing, the kind that demanded not only skill but also a well of compassion that could easily run dry. Oklahoma City, on the other hand, came with a job description that was hazy at best. The offer was filled with assurances— "we'll find a role for you," "there's a place waiting"—but no specifics. It was a leap into the unknown.

In the end, I chose Oklahoma City. I packed my bags and returned to the familiar streets of my childhood, clinging to the hope that I was making the right decision. And while it would ultimately lead me to blessings I could not yet see, it also ushered me into one of the darkest valleys of my life.

The organization I joined in Oklahoma City was not a stranger to me. I had grown up knowing its name, its history, and some of the people who ran it. Executives and board members had been family acquaintances, men and women I had looked up to from afar. But when I arrived, the job I was handed was far beneath anything I had envisioned. I wasn't given an office, a title, or even meaningful responsibilities. Instead, I was placed in the workshop, assigned to tasks so monotonous they could have been completed by machines: folding shower curtains, packaging medical supplies, and assembling fire hoses. Day after day, my hands moved automatically, but my heart sank a little lower. I hated it.

It felt like drowning in slow motion. I had carried dreams of leadership, of ministry, of meaningful work that would challenge and stretch me. Instead, I found myself swallowed up by repetition and disappointment. My coworkers were not people I would have chosen for myself. Many came from vastly different backgrounds—rougher edges, harder stories. At first, they looked at me with suspicion, convinced I was some "rich kid" planted there to watch them, to report back, or to climb past them on the ladder. I felt their eyes on me every time I entered the room, every time I opened my mouth. But over time, as days bled into weeks, we began to understand each other. We found common ground in small jokes, in the rhythm of the work, in the unspoken camaraderie of people stuck in the same grind. Slowly, tolerance grew, and eventually, a kind of respect.

Yet, no matter how much I tried to accept it, the job I had been promised never came. I applied for other roles within the organization, positions where I thought my skills and passion could be used. Each time, I received polite but firm rejections—phrased in that professional language that cuts deeper than outright dismissal. "Not the right fit." "Perhaps at a later time." "We appreciate your interest." Each no felt like an open door slammed shut inches from my face.

During this season, I often thought about King David. Before the throne, before the crown, there was the wilderness. David had been anointed, chosen by God, yet he spent years hiding from Saul, wandering caves and deserts, living in the tension between the promise and the reality. That was me. I knew I had a calling. I knew God had planted something greater in my life. But instead of stepping into it, I was folding shower curtains. Like David, I was learning resilience in the shadows, humility in the silence, and patience in the waiting. But knowing that didn't make the valley any less painful. Each day felt like dodging arrows of doubt and discouragement.

There was, however, one small bright spot. The workshop occasionally hosted tours for visitors, and one of my friends invited me to help lead them. That became my lifeline. Guiding people through the space, explaining the mission of the organization, highlighting the overlooked skills of the workers—it sparked something in me again. I came alive in those moments. I loved connecting with strangers, watching their faces light up when they understood the bigger picture. On a few occasions, politicians and community leaders walked through, and though I didn't seize the opportunity to know them personally, those encounters reminded me of who I was and who I could still become. It was a glimpse of purpose amid the monotony.

Eventually, my persistence paid off, and I was moved into a new role—closer to the kind of work I had dreamed of doing. I thought at last the waiting was over, the wilderness behind me. But life has a way of surprising us, often at the most unexpected times. On the very first official day of that role, I received a text message that would alter the trajectory of everything. It was the spark of a dream I had long since buried, suddenly breathing again, coming alive in a way I could not have imagined.

The valley season was not over, not by a long shot. The path ahead was still rugged. The winds still whipped hard against me. But for the first time in a long time, I could see a break in the storm clouds. The faintest trace of blue sky was beginning to appear, and with it came hope—hope that the valley was not the end of my story, but the place where God was preparing me for the mountaintop that lay ahead.

Take Away:

Chasing your dreams means walking through valleys or seasons of disappointment and uncertainty, when things feel far from what you can see. During those times, preparation is happening for what comes next.

Dreams have a way of stirring excitement in us, almost like fireflies flickering in the night — small but radiant sparks that hint at what's possible. But chasing those dreams rarely looks like the glossy highlight reels we scroll past online. It looks more like valleys. It looks like silence. It looks like working in a workshop that smells like oil and iron while your heart aches for a future that feels a thousand miles away.

The valleys are the price of admission to the mountaintop.

We don't like valleys. Let's be honest: no one ever prays for them. We want open doors, red carpets, glowing signs from heaven with arrows pointing "this way to success." Instead, life slams doors in our face — sometimes with enough force to rattle our bones. We are left standing there, clutching rejection slips or staring at a silent inbox that refuses to yield any good news. And it's in those moments that the real test begins: will you give up because the door didn't open, or will you keep knocking even when it feels like no one is on the other side?

For me, the valley felt like a season of delay. I was waiting on a text message that could change everything, a single spark that could shift the entire direction of my life. I prayed. I fasted. I believed. And yet, the silence persisted. Days dragged into weeks, weeks into months, and the waiting pressed heavy on my chest like a weight I couldn't shake off. That's what the wilderness feels like — the in-between, where your prayers seem to echo back empty. And yet, strangely, it's also where faith grows its deepest roots.

Romans 12:12 says, "Rejoice in our confident hope Be patient in trouble and keep on praying." That's not just a verse you underline neatly in your Bible and move on from. It's not a motivational bumper sticker. It's a verse you live when your hope feels paper-thin, when affliction is your daily bread, and when prayer feels like an unanswered voicemail left on God's machine. It's not about faking joy or plastering on a smile. It's about choosing, daily, to anchor yourself in the belief that silence does not equal abandonment. Silence can mean preparation.

Preparation rarely looks like success. More often, it looks like failure. It looks like being stuck in a workshop when your heart longs to be in a classroom, a stage, a boardroom, or wherever your passion lives. It looks like friends moving forward — promotions, marriages, families, opportunities — while you feel like you're standing still. It looks like jobs that don't reflect your calling, routines that feel empty, and days that feel wasted. And yet, here's the hidden truth: nothing in the valley is wasted.

Think of David in Scripture. Before he became king, he was anointed — chosen by God Himself through the prophet Samuel. And yet, immediately after, he went back to the sheep. Not to the throne. Not to the palace. Not to a military post. Back to the fields, smelling of sheep. Imagine the whiplash of that reality. The promise of kingship in his pocket, but his hands still rough with the work of tending animals. That was David's valley. And yet, it was in those fields that he learned courage — facing lions and bears. It was in those lonely spaces that he learned to worship, playing the harp until his music was strong enough to soothe a tormented king. Those hidden years, those forgotten seasons, became his preparation for the crown.

And the same is true for us. Your workshop days, your hidden days, your silent days — they are sharpening you in ways you can't yet see. When the door finally swings open, you'll realize the valley was your training ground.

But the valley isn't only about endurance. It's also about honesty. During that chapter of my life, my prayers became raw. They weren't polished or eloquent. They sounded less like carefully crafted sermons and more like broken confessions. "God, are You hearing me? Why does it feel like You've forgotten me?" I was half ashamed to pray like that — until I realized God already knew the condition of my heart. The valley doesn't require perfect prayers. It requires honest ones.

And in that honesty, you learn dependence. The kind of dependence that makes you lean into faith when nothing else makes sense. The kind that forces you to seek wisdom from mentors, encouragement from friends, and truth from Scripture. Alone, valleys can crush us. But with a few trusted people walking beside you, they become bearable. That's why community matters so much. That's why you need friends who won't just pat you on the back but will remind you of Romans 12:12 when you're tempted to forget.

One of the cruelest lies of the valley is the belief that you are alone in it. But the truth is, every dreamer has walked through their own valley. Every leader has faced silence and uncertainty. Every person chasing something greater has endured seasons where nothing seemed to add up. The valley is not punishment. It's not failure. It's part of the curriculum.

And here's where the strange beauty comes in: the valley shifts your vision. It changes the way you see. You start noticing the small, overlooked glimpses of grace in the monotony. A co-worker's unexpected kindness. A laugh shared in the middle of an otherwise heavy day. A sliver of sunlight cutting through a gray morning. These aren't the victories you prayed for, but they are reminders — breadcrumbs along the trail — that you haven't been abandoned.

So, what do you do in the valley?

You keep showing up. Even when it doesn't feel like it matters. Because showing up is an act of rebellion against despair. You pray, even when your words feel empty, because prayer keeps the line open. You stay patient in affliction — not passive, but patient — because you trust that unseen growth is happening beneath the soil of your struggle.

Progress almost always starts with the smallest, humblest steps. Walking into another workshop shift. Cracking open the Bible again. Sending another application. Whispering another prayer. None of these things look dramatic. None of them feel like breakthroughs. But persistence doesn't guarantee immediate results — it guarantees alignment with the possibility of doors opening in the future.

And the valley? It isn't forever. Doors that slam shut today can swing wide tomorrow. Silence you endure now can echo later as songs of testimony. That is the promise of hope — not that you'll avoid valleys, but that you'll be strengthened through them.

So if you find yourself in a valley right now — staring at slammed doors, unanswered prayers, or long days that feel empty — remember this: you are not stuck. You are being shaped. Chasing your dreams does mean walking through disappointment and uncertainty. But those seasons are never wasted. They are molding you into someone who will not only reach the dream, but sustain it when it arrives.

Rejoice in our confident hope Be patient in trouble and keep on praying.". Romans 12:12 is not just a verse to memorize. It's a survival guide for the valley. More than that — it's the blueprint for walking out of the valley stronger, with deeper roots, and with a faith that can carry the weight of the mountaintop.

CHAPTER 10

Never Say Never

Remember earlier when I said those fateful words, "I never"? Well, like my mom and Granny always warned, "Never say never." Life has a way of circling back to test the vows we make, especially the ones we cling to with the most stubbornness. By this point, I was already working for an organization that employed people with disabilities, something I once thought I'd never do. And now, the second "never"—as in, I would never go back to school for a master's degree—was creeping up fast behind me like an unwelcome guest.

It was the summer of 2020 when I received a phone call that would shake the certainty of that "never." The call came from the quirky, unforgettable Orientation and Mobility Specialist who had once helped me navigate the campus at UCO. Over the years, we had kept in touch, and I had even spoken at a few of her transition events for blind students. This time, though, she wasn't just calling to check in—she was calling with a heads-up. A position would soon be opening in her office. She didn't know exactly when, but she encouraged me to keep an eye out for it.

The truth was, my heart was already set on working for that agency. The problem? There were no openings, and every role required a master's degree. That was the barrier standing between me and the calling I felt tugging at my soul. And so, with hesitation and a deep swallow of pride, I did what I once said I'd never do: I started researching graduate programs in Visual Rehabilitation Therapy. I sat down with countless pros-and-cons lists, prayed over my options, and after much soul-searching, I landed on a university in Western Michigan. For the first time in years, I dared to consider becoming a student again.

I hadn't been in school for what felt like forever, and the thought of entering a master's program filled me with dread. A friend tried to reassure me by saying graduate-level courses were more interesting than undergrad. He was right. They were more engaging, but also more demanding. There were nights I wondered if I had the stamina to endure it. But doors don't open unless you knock, and I was determined to knock.

In December of that year, I got a message from Debi: "The job's up. Apply now." My heart jumped. I applied immediately, and by March of 2021—just two months into my master's program—I was officially working for the state agency that would become such a defining part of my success.

Now, let me tell you: pursuing a master's degree is already challenging. Doing it while working full-time? That's a mountain climb with no breaks for air. My days became a blur of work, paperwork, studying, writing, and more studying. I'd go to work all day, come home, and bury myself in assignments late into the night. Was it hard? Absolutely. Did I want to quit? More times than I can count. But beneath the exhaustion lived a deep gratitude, because I knew how rare this opportunity was.

When I applied for the job, I didn't know the territory I would cover. It turned out to be the entire southwestern region of Oklahoma, including the very town where my family lived. At first, I didn't fully understand the scope of the role. I just knew I'd be helping people adjust to life with vision loss. What I didn't expect was the mountain of paperwork—case notes, initial assessments, progress reports. At the time, it felt overwhelming. Ironically, that paperwork has now become one of my favorite parts of the job. I can knock out a case note or intake summary in minutes, something that once took hours of second-guessing.

But don't mistake that for an easy journey. None of it came naturally. I had a supervisor I respected deeply, though at times it felt like I could never measure up in her eyes. She was tough, with high expectations and sharp feedback. I questioned almost every email she sent, replayed her words in my head, and often doubted myself. But I realize now how much she shaped me. She taught me how to write with efficiency, precision, and professionalism. By my first performance review, I had earned high marks, and for the first time, I felt an undeniable sense of belonging. I knew: this was where I was meant to be.

Our work in the field goes far beyond teaching people how to live without sight. We walk with them through grief. We sit with their families as they navigate shock and fear. We help them realize that blindness, while life-altering, is not the end. Back in my undergrad years, I had taken a Psychology of Grief class just to fill a credit. Little did I know how vital that class would become. Today, it undergirds so much of my work, as I guide clients and families through their darkest days. It's the most rewarding part of what I do—helping people realize that blindness isn't a final sentence, but a new beginning.

Meanwhile, graduate school came with its own tests. Some classes were brutal. Anatomy of the eye was one of my favorites, though it stretched my brain in ways I hadn't experienced in years. I also had professors who clashed with my writing style, pushing me to refine my voice. And finally, on May 5th, 2023, after endless nights of writing, reading, and doubting myself, I completed my coursework. I was officially done with school—or so I thought.

Because finishing classes wasn't the end. I still needed to pass the national certification exam. And that exam became my Goliath. I tried five times. Five. Each time, I came up short. Some failures sting for a day; this one lingered. Like a coxswain guiding their crew through choppy waters, I tried to steer myself through, but the waves kept pulling me under. Each attempt tested my resilience, forcing me to face the question: How badly do I want this? The answer, each time, was the same—I want it enough to keep trying.

One thing has become clear: I am a fierce advocate for people who are blind. This job has deepened that passion. I want the world to see that blindness is not a disability—it's an inconvenience. Blind people can do almost anything anyone else can do; sometimes, they just need to take a different path to get there. If I see barriers, I'll do everything in my power to knock them down. My drive is not just professional—it's personal. I want a world where blindness does not mean limitation.

Professionally, this journey has changed me. I've grown in resilience, maturity, and adaptability. I've learned how to thrive in a predominantly female office environment, embracing the dynamics and perspectives that come with it. I've grown curious about how every department of our agency operates, always seeking new challenges. And, true to my Enneagram Type 3 nature, I confess: I need to achieve. Standing still isn't an option.

I love my coworkers. Do I always like them in the moment? Not always. But I love them, because they are my crew. They push me, support me, and remind me why I'm here.

A coworker spoke to me about how much I have in common with Jonah and the whale. I was running—running from working with people with disabilities, running from my call, even running from myself. But God had other plans. He brought me right back to the place I said I'd never be, teaching me that His plans are not derailed by our "nevers."

In this role, I've met people I never would have crossed paths with otherwise—people who have reshaped my understanding of resilience and faith. Looking back, I see now that my earlier experiences at the other organization, working with underserved and economically challenged communities, were not wasted years. They were preparation. I was learning to meet people where they were, to listen, to bridge differences, and to connect with those whose lives looked nothing like mine.

And that, more than anything, has made all the difference.

Take Away:

Never say never, especially when God has other plans for you. Keep walking through any door that is open; you never know where it would lead.

We all have those moments when we think we have life figured out, when we look at the world and make firm statements like, "I'll never do that," or "I'll never go there." It's a kind of self-preservation, an attempt to draw boundaries around our lives and our expectations. We convince ourselves that by saying never, we are asserting control over our futures. But life has a way of laughing at our certainty, reminding us that what we think we know is only a fraction of the plan.

That truth hit me squarely. I had long believed that pursuing a master's degree was off the table for me — a clear, non-negotiable boundary. Yet, in a twist I could not have anticipated, that door opened. God had other plans. The opportunity did not arrive with fanfare or a neon sign pointing the way; it arrived in a quiet phone call, in a reminder from someone who had always believed in me. It came wrapped in the challenge of balancing graduate school with a full-time job — a daunting prospect that I had confidently told myself I would never take on. And yet, it became the doorway to a chapter I never could have scripted.

Here, the lesson is not about education or career alone; it's about openness. Never is not an unbreakable wall. It is a placeholder for our own limited vision. When God, or life itself, has other plans, those plans often come through doors we had not been watching, doors that may appear inconvenient or impossible at first glance. But every open door is an invitation to step into the unknown — to embrace potential, growth, and opportunities we hadn't imagined. Walking through requires courage, yes, but also humility: humility to admit we do not know everything, humility to trust the timing, and humility to accept that our previous assumptions about what we could or could not do were often too small.

Entering that master's program while starting a full-time career was an exercise in trust, persistence, and patience. It demanded long days and longer nights, constant adjustments, and the steadying knowledge that progress was incremental. Yet, as difficult as it was, the experience reaffirmed a critical truth: doors that align with your purpose may not be convenient, comfortable, or predictable. They might demand more than you expected to give. They might require sacrifice. They might ask you to stretch beyond the limits you have imposed on yourself. But stepping through them, rather than remaining rigid in our "never" declarations, is where transformation begins.

There is also a humility in never saying never. It forces us to confront the limits of our foresight and the arrogance of our assumptions. I had said I would never pursue graduate school, yet here I was, thriving in a role that had previously seemed unattainable without that exact qualification. Life has a way of orchestrating outcomes that surpass our imagination, but only if we are willing to step through doors we hadn't planned for. Saying never closes those doors preemptively; walking through them opens a space for divine timing and unforeseen blessings to manifest.

Also, never say never is a reminder about flexibility in ambition. Our goals, our dreams, our "perfect plans" — they are often just frameworks, not fixed outcomes. When doors open in unexpected ways, they may lead to paths that look different than what we imagined, but still fulfill our purpose. The mastery comes not in rigidly clinging to our preconceptions but in embracing the unpredictability of life's design. In my case, pursuing the master's degree while starting my career reshaped my understanding of possibility, capacity, and faith. It taught me that what seems impossible today may become the foundation for tomorrow's achievements.

In the broader sense, this lesson extends beyond personal ambition. Open doors present chances to connect, to serve, to influence, and to grow in ways that cannot be measured solely by immediate outcomes. Each opportunity invites us to stretch beyond comfort zones, navigate challenges, and refine our character. They remind us that life's plans are often larger and more intricate than our own. And they remind us to approach the world with humility, curiosity, and a readiness to learn from every doorway we encounter.

Never say never also speaks to persistence. Doors may open only a crack at first; you may need to push, step forward, or accept discomfort before fully entering. Opportunities often arrive in fragments — a call, an email, a suggestion, a recommendation — rather than fully formed offers. But recognizing these as the openings they are, and committing to walk through them, allows us to convert potential into tangible progress. Persistence ensures that the moments we might otherwise dismiss become meaningful turning points.

In practical terms, this philosophy is deceptively simple: keep moving, keep observing, and keep accepting what life presents with openness. The summer phone call from Debi, the encouragement from mentors, the support network I had cultivated over the years — each was a door inviting me to step forward, even when I had previously told myself that I wouldn't. And stepping through these doors brought unforeseen alignment between my education, career, and personal growth. It reinforced that the "never" we impose on ourselves is often the very barrier preventing us from entering the spaces we were meant to inhabit.

Ultimately, Never say never is not just a cliché; it's a directive for navigating life's uncertainty. It's a call to remain open to the opportunities that arise unexpectedly, to honor the plans that may surpass our comprehension, and to trust that what appears as a challenge may, in fact, be the doorway to fulfillment. The open doors — those invitations from life, faith, or circumstance — are rarely obvious in their significance. Only by walking through them do we begin to understand their purpose.

Never say never also teaches patience. Doors may not open when we want them to, and opportunities may arrive in ways we do not anticipate. The timing may feel inconvenient, the requirements daunting, and the expectations steep. Yet, when we answer the call, when we step forward despite uncertainty, we engage with life's rhythm rather than resist it. And in doing so, we often discover that what we initially feared is precisely what we needed all along.

I do not know what door will be opened next for me but I'm ready to walk through it.

As you navigate your own journey, remember this: never say never. Keep walking through any door that is open, even if it leads somewhere unexpected. Trust that the pathways you didn't plan for, the challenges you feared, and the opportunities you hadn't imagined may collectively shape a life richer and fuller than you could have predicted. Open doors are invitations to grow, to learn, to serve, and to fulfill the potential that God has placed within you. Step forward. Keep walking. And let the doors you never expected guide you to the life you were meant to lead.

CHAPTER 11

Anchored in Faith and Connections

One thing that most people will say about me is that I know a plethora of people. My friends and coworkers often joke that I know everyone. And while it's true that I have met and connected with many people over the years, I don't see myself as someone who knows everyone—nor would I want to. What I do know is the value of connection, of community, and of showing up for people in ways that matter. I love meeting people, learning their stories, and, when possible, connecting them to someone else who can help them accomplish their goals or overcome obstacles. To me, there is something sacred about being a bridge for others, about creating networks of support and encouragement in a world that can often feel isolating.

I try to approach everyone with loyalty and respect. It's a principle I hold dearly. However, honesty is also a non-negotiable for me. I'm not one to sugarcoat the truth when someone needs to hear it—but I also guard my trust carefully. If someone does something that causes me to lose faith in them, then, unfortunately, they will not find a place in my inner circle again. Trust is precious, and once broken, it's nearly impossible to rebuild. Yet, I remain open to giving people chances when they are willing to prove themselves worthy, because I understand that we are all works in progress.

Reflecting on my journey, one thing that continues to amaze me is how God places people in our lives for a specific time and purpose. I've come to see that these seasons of connection are not random—they are intentional, orchestrated, and perfectly timed. God, being all-knowing, positions individuals in our lives to help guide us, support us, and sometimes challenge us, even when we don't fully understand why at the moment. I have questioned His motives many times, wondering why certain doors were closed or why certain people came and went. Yet each time, I have had to walk with faith, trusting that He is in control and that His timing is flawless, even when mine feels impatient.

Let me give an example of this. One day, I received a phone call from an old friend who I hadn't spoken to in years. He asked me to review a popular app to help make it more accessible for people who are blind or have low vision. I gladly agreed. As I tested the app, I found a few areas that were difficult to navigate. I sent him a quick, detailed message highlighting the issues, and he responded promptly, promising to implement changes. That brief interaction reminded me that even small connections can have a meaningful impact. It's a perfect example of God using people at just the right time, positioning them to help me—and me to help others.

The fall of 2023 was a remarkable season. I could see that all the work I had invested in over the years was beginning to bear fruit. Back in 2021, I had been asked to appear in PSA ads for our agency, and in 2023, I was asked to film a new PSA for the upcoming year. It was a public acknowledgment that the contributions I had made were being seen and appreciated. That same year, I was honored as one of Oklahoma City's most Influential Young Professionals. Receiving the Frontline Award through Oklahoma Workforce, as well as being named Public Personnel Employee of the Year by the Oklahoma City Mayor's Council for Disability Concern, was both humbling and affirming. Recognition is not the reason I do what I do, but these moments serve as milestones, reminders that perseverance, dedication, and faithfulness matter.

In addition to these achievements, I also joined Toastmasters that year. My goal was to better engage with audiences and grow as a public speaker. I knew that the ability to communicate clearly, persuasively, and empathetically could make a tangible difference in my work and advocacy for people who are blind or low vision. Toastmasters provided a structured environment to hone these skills, challenge my comfort zones, and learn from others who were equally committed to personal and professional growth. It reminded me that growth is continuous, and that learning doesn't stop—even when we've reached milestones we once thought unattainable.

As you read through this book, you might find yourself thinking, "Wow! This guy has lived so much in just thirty-four years." And yes, you are correct. But I did not navigate this journey alone. I had a great crew walking beside me every step of the way—friends, family, mentors, colleagues, and even acquaintances who became guides during critical moments. Life is rarely a solo expedition, and I've learned that surrounding yourself with people who genuinely care, who challenge you to grow, and who believe in you even when you struggle, is vital.

I haven't shared every low season in my life—there are chapters I've left private, moments that remain tucked away in my heart. Those experiences shaped me quietly, preparing me for the higher seasons. They were seasons of learning patience, resilience, and humility. Yet, even in those moments, I never felt entirely alone. My anchor has always been my faith, my family, my friends, and yes, my stubborn determination to keep moving forward no matter how rough the waters.

Faith has been central to my journey. It has been the steady foundation through storms of doubt, fear, and uncertainty. My belief that God is orchestrating every season, placing people strategically in my life, has allowed me to navigate challenges with hope instead of despair. Even when I questioned His methods or timing, I learned to rest in the knowledge that His plans are greater than mine. Trusting in that truth has been liberating, even when the path was unclear or the waters turbulent.

Family has been another crucial anchor. Their unwavering support, encouragement, and occasional tough love have grounded me. Family is not just the people related to you by blood—it's those who show up, invest in your growth, and cheer you on, even when the road seems impossible. They have celebrated victories with me, lifted me when I stumbled, and reminded me that my story is not just my own, but part of a larger tapestry of relationships and experiences.

Friends have played an equally important role. Each person I've met, whether briefly or for many years, has left a mark. Some have been mentors, offering guidance and perspective I couldn't find anywhere else. Others have been cheerleaders, giving me the confidence to pursue opportunities I might otherwise have doubted. And then there are those who challenged me, who tested my patience, resilience, and faith—but even those relationships were instrumental. God often places people in our lives to teach us lessons, and sometimes those lessons come in the form of confrontation, challenge, or even disappointment.

Finally, there is the stubbornness, the "thick head" as I like to call it, that has kept me moving forward. It's the inner drive that refuses to let obstacles dictate my direction. It's the quiet rebellion against giving up, the persistence that says, "I will keep showing up. I will keep learning. I will keep walking through doors that are open, even if I don't know where they will lead." That stubbornness, tempered by faith and grounded in community, has been essential in navigating the valleys, the storms, and the seasons of growth.

One of the greatest truths I have learned is that God's timing is perfect, even when it feels delayed. The people He places in our lives are never random—they are strategically positioned to guide, support, challenge, and teach us. Reflecting on the past years, I can see clearly how every interaction, every connection, and every relationship served a purpose. Whether it was helping me navigate professional spaces, supporting my advocacy efforts, or encouraging personal growth, these relationships were all integral to the life I am living now.

So, as this book comes to a close, I hope you take away this message: life is rarely linear, and success is rarely solitary. The people you meet, the connections you build, and the faith you maintain during difficult seasons are what enable you to navigate life's rough waters. Your anchor—whether it is faith, family, friends, or your own determination—will carry you through. Trust in the process, even when you cannot see the outcome. Keep walking through the doors that are open, and never underestimate the power of those God places in your path for a season.

No matter what challenges you face, no matter how rough the waters, no matter how many times you are tempted to turn back, remember that you are not alone. There is a crew walking with you. There is an anchor that will not fail. There are doors yet to open. There is purpose yet to be fulfilled. And when you look back one day, you will see that every season, every connection, every challenge was preparing you for exactly where you are meant to be.

Take Away:

The Power of Connections and Faith Through Life's Rough Waters

You know, life has this funny way of showing us who really matters, and when. People come into our lives for a reason, a season, or sometimes just a brief moment that leaves an impact we can't quite explain. I've been thinking a lot about that lately, about how God has this way of positioning people in your life at exactly the right time—sometimes before you even know you need them, sometimes when you're in the middle of a storm you thought you'd never survive. It's crazy how the right conversation, the right introduction, or even just a simple text from an old friend can change your entire perspective.

I've always loved meeting people. You could say I know a lot of people—or at least, people tell me I do—but it's not about the numbers for me. It's about connection. It's about loyalty, respect, and honesty. And let me be clear: I'm honest to a fault. I'll give it to you straight. But that also means if you betray my trust, there's no coming back. I've had to learn that the hard way. And yet, despite my thick head and stubborn pride, I've realized something: the people God places in your life aren't there to make you comfortable—they're there to help you navigate, to guide you, to show you parts of yourself you didn't even know existed.

Take the example of my old friend who reached out one day asking me to review an app. He knew I'd have insight as someone who is blind or low vision. Simple, right? But that small interaction was more than a favor. It was a reminder that my experience, my perspective, and even the struggles I've faced—all of it—has value. And it's a perfect example of how connections work. Sometimes it's not about the big moments or the awards. Sometimes it's about a phone call, a message, a nod of recognition. That connection is God's way of saying, "You're not alone in this."

And speaking of recognition, let's not forget the bigger milestones. The fall of 2023 was wild. Looking back, I realized that all the work I'd done, all the small, persistent efforts in different areas of my life, had been paying off. From filming PSA ads for our agency to being named one of Oklahoma City's most Influential Young Professionals, to receiving the Frontline Award through Oklahoma

Workforce and the Public Personnel Employee of the Year award from the Mayor's Council for Disability Concern—each moment was a reminder that perseverance, faith, and the right people in your corner matter.

Even joining Toastmasters that same year, just to refine my speaking skills, was a strategic move. Not because I wanted to check a box or add a title, but because I recognized the value of investing in myself while leaning on a community that encouraged growth. Those connections—friends, mentors, coworkers, even casual acquaintances—made all the difference in shaping the person I am today.

See, here's the thing about faith: it isn't just a blanket of comfort or a ticket out of hardship. It's an anchor, a compass, and sometimes a lifeline when the waters get rough. When I say "rough waters," I don't just mean big, obvious storms. I mean the small, quiet ones that gnaw at you over time—the moments when doors slam shut, when opportunities seem to vanish, when you're waiting for a text or a call that may never come. That's when your faith matters most. That's when your community matters most.

I've learned that faith and connections work hand in hand. Alone, faith can feel like hope with no visible path. And connections without faith can feel empty. But when the two come together—when you trust that God has a plan while walking alongside people who lift, guide, and challenge you—the impossible starts to feel reachable. You realize that no moment, no struggle, no relationship is wasted. Even the hard ones teach you something: resilience, humility, patience, discernment.

I want you to understand this clearly: the anchor isn't just something you have when life is calm. The anchor is what keeps you grounded when waves are crashing around you. For me, my anchor has always been faith, family, friends, and yes, my thick head that refuses to quit. And the people God places in your life? They are like additional anchors, ropes thrown out to help steady you, guide you, or even just remind you that someone else has your back.

And let's not shy away from the truth: not everyone is going to stay. People will come and go, and that's okay. That doesn't mean the connection was meaningless. It just means their season in your life was specific. Some lessons are meant to be brief but impactful. Some friendships are meant to challenge you, to shake you awake, or to push you forward. And when those seasons end, your faith and the lessons you've learned are what keep you moving forward.

In reflecting on my journey, I can honestly say I wouldn't be who I am today without the crew that God has placed in my life. The people who challenged me, encouraged me, held me accountable, and even the ones who simply believed in me when I doubted myself—they shaped my path. And that path, with all its twists and turns, triumphs and setbacks, has shown me something crucial: it's not about avoiding the rough waters. It's about learning how to navigate them, knowing you have an anchor and a network to guide you through.

So here's my challenge to you: take stock of your own life. Look at the people you've encountered, the relationships that have lifted you, and the moments that seemed small but ended up being monumental. See the fingerprints of God in those connections. Recognize that your faith, paired with the right community, is a powerhouse. It can steady you, inspire you, and carry you when you feel like giving up.

And finally, understand this: your journey is ongoing. Life doesn't hand you a map with every detail. Sometimes, you have to walk blindly, trusting that each step is bringing you closer to where you're meant to be. But when you anchor yourself in faith and lean on the people God has placed in your life, the rough waters become navigable. The storms don't disappear, but you learn to ride them. You learn to see the value in the struggle. You learn that every connection, every act of loyalty, every bit of honesty—those are all tools for survival and growth.

So, as you close this book, I want you to remember: the power of connections and faith is real. It's not theoretical. It's not abstract. It's the thing that makes rough waters bearable, that makes you resilient, that allows you to keep going even when the current is strong. Hold onto your anchor. Treasure your crew. Walk in faith. And never underestimate the people God places in your life for a season—they may very well be the reason you make it through, the reason you thrive, and the reason you finally reach that shore you've been seeking all along.

Made in United States
Orlando, FL
23 November 2025